Monk
in the mountain

Questions from the city, answers from the forest.

Ajahn Sumano Bhikkhu

"Nothing is better than something. "0" is the pointless point; therefore it is superior to any number. When your karma has been eradicated, there is nothing. It takes considerable wisdom to want to be nothing."

Ajahn Sumano Bhikkhu

Ajahn Sumamo Bhikkhu
P.O. Box3, Glang Dong, Nakorn Ratchasima 30320
Fax: +66 44 935 596
Email: monksumano@yahoo.com
Website: www.next-life.com

Author:	Ajahn Sumano Bhikkhu
Publisher:	Tam Song Ta Meditation Sanctuary
	(Double Eyed Cave)

Editor	Dithaya Punyaratabandhu
Proofreader	Elly Edelhoff-Oglesby
	Supakrith Punyaratabandhu
	Sivalee Anantachart

Creative & Artwork	Athtapon Korapoom
Print Coordinator	Wanida Phadungphong
Photographer	Onuma Prommin
Project Coordinator	Kusira Punyaratabandhu

Printed at:	LOL Ad House Co., Ltd.
	6/39 Chokchai 4 Soi 22
	Ladprao, Bangkok 10230

Second Edition, September 2010
5000 copies

ISBN: 978-0-615-25061-8

Printed in Thailand

6 Monk in the mountain

Introduction

By Roy Hamric, Chiang Mai, Thailand

The Monk in the Double-Eyed Cave

"Lonely and quiet places,
Haunts of deer and wild beasts
Should the Bhikkhu seek as his abode
For solitude's sweet sake."
– From "Questions To King Milanda."

My friend mentioned a *thudong* monk, an American, who had lived in a cave alone for more than 15 years. "Oh, he also has e-mail and a Website," he said. The monk was in the *thudong* lineage, the most revered in Thailand. *Thudong* monks are wandering, meditating monks who try to follow the strict rules set down by the Buddha 2,600 years ago. Just the word *thudong* evokes a powerful picture in the mind of a Thai: a barefoot monk walking along backroad or jungle paths, carrying an alms bowl, a big grot (a large umbrella with mosquito netting that unfolds and sets up at night to make a tent-like enclosure), and a cloth shoulder bag. The shoulder bag might contain a few simple items: matches, razors, a sewing kit, drinking cup, candles, a water filter and some Buddhist scriptures.

The master *thudong* monks of the past wandered through the pristine jungles and forests of Thailand. They encouraged their young disciples to take up solitary residence in isolated caves, or under the canopy of large trees, or in cemeteries or charnel grounds. It was traditional for *thudong* monks, when entering villages, to set up their grot in cemeteries, to the amazement of local residents who were fearful of evil spirits.

"*Ajahn*" means teacher. *Sumano* means "good heart" in Pali. "*Bhikkhu*" means 'one who is striving to come to the end of the world'. My friend said Ajahn Sumano Bhikkhu was a genuine monk who followed entirely the 227 rules which were established by the Buddha himself, a monk who maintained a strict and disciplined meditation practice. I e-mailed Sumano Bhikkhu and a few days later my car was bouncing down a red-dirt road running parallel to a ripening corn field about 100 kilometers northeast of Bangkok in Khao Yai Mountain. The outline of a picket fence appeared in the distance, running parallel to a small mountain covered by dense trees and foliage. The road passed through a gate and dead-ended in front of a cave about mid-way up the mountain.

Orange robes fluttered on the clothes line. Behind the line a rock path led up the mountain to the cave.

Sumano Bhikkhu, broom in hand, stopped sweeping leaves and smiled. He walked over gracefully. From a distance, he looked like a very large man. At a certain angle, his face and nose recalled the famous, imposing drawing of Boddhidharma, but his eyes had a friendly, happy glint, as perhaps Boddhidharma's did too. White hair stubble covered his shaved head like a fine powder. Dangling from the back of his neck was a 6-inch strip of green tape.

"I'm experimenting with a Chinese herbal plaster that's supposed to help the elements get into perfect harmony," Sumano said, grinning.

After the friendly formalities, we sat on meditation pads in a shaded terrace where he receives visitors. I handed him my card.

"Wait a minute, in Thailand even the street sweepers have a card," he said, digging into his rumpled shoulder bag. As I studied his card, complete with his color photograph and his e-mail and website addresses, he punched my address into his hand-held electronic organizer.

He had lived in Double-Eyed Cave since 1991. At age 67, he still walked a five-mile alms round each morning and ate only one meal a day. When he was younger, he roamed around Thailand, Malaysia and India, experiencing the same physical and mental hardships of earlier *thudong* monks. Now he was living a much different life, but still rigorously practicing meditation. He was a senior monk now, having passed more than 25 rain retreats, the three-month period when *thudong* monks gather together to practice extended meditation. Over the past seven years, he has written three books on a battery-powered second hand Mac laptop. A Thai disciple in Bangkok designed and maintains his website. I asked about the tug between solitude and worldy activity here at his cave retreat.

"I have just enough visitors here at the cave to emphasize and underline the struggle in the unenlightened human condition," he said. "Let's go up and you can see where I live."

A sign at the trailhead gate read: the Rules of Double-Eyed Cave:

Visiting hours 8-10 a.m.; 5-8 p.m.

One meal a day at 8 a.m.

Do not offer money (except in an envelope)

Kindly be quiet in this area

Women must be accompanied by a man

Do not enter unless you have business with the monk

The monk does not accept invitations.

"Villagers told me that a tiger lived in this cave before a monk finally moved in before me," Sumano Bhikku said, as we climbed the 200-foot stone trail. The cave entrance was 20-feet high, with a 6-foot stone wall and double doors forming a protective entryway. Inside, the sunlight dimmed to an amber glow and faded to black 50 feet beyond. We were in a large cave chamber with a level floor. On the right side, a smaller, second cave entrance sent a narrow, slanting sunbeam into the darkness – the other "eye" of the Double-Eyed Cave.

Musty air carried a sweet smell of incense. Stone tiles paved the cave's floor area. Cloth meditation cushions and straw mats lay scattered about. A single-burner propane stove sat on counter area, and a large propane fuel tank powered a heating plate for tea. A white-gas lantern served as a night light. Clothes and non-perishable items were stored in sealed plastic containers. "The containers keep out insects, rats and snakes," Sumano Bhikkhu said.

A 4-foot plaster Buddha statue rested atop a raised platform in the center of the living chamber. Photographs of several renowned *thudong* masters, Ajahn (Teacher) Mun and Ajahn Chaa, Ajahn Tate, and Ajahn Buddhadasa rested at the base of the Buddha. Sumano Bhikkhu formally received guests while sitting on a cushion at the base of the Buddha platform. Plastic bottles of drinking water, two large Thai-English dictionaries and a Phillips battery-powered, cassette recorder-player lay next to his meditation cushion. A 40-foot walking meditation path made of fine sand lay off to the right. Behind the meditation path was a space for yoga and a few more metal storage cabinets for candles and incense. Along the farthest wall was a raised platform where sleeping pads could be placed.

"Let's go down to another meditation area," he said, picking up a flashlight. We walked down hand-hewed steps cut into the rock into a black darkness and then circled back to the right. The flashlight beam illuminated two wood sleeping platforms along the far wall of a sunken pit.

"This is the area where I usually come to rest," Sumano Bhikkhu said. "I've seen cobras in this area – two of them – they slither by now and again. That's why I raised the bed with bricks."

"It was high counsel that I once heard given to a young person— 'Always do what you are afraid to do.'" --Emerson, Heroism Essay

Stories abound about the exploits of *thudong* monks in Thailand. *Thudong* monks are expected to use their fear, their loneliness, their deepest doubts, and their daily struggle as a constant mental practice, to deepen their understanding of how the mind works. The master teachers were very clear about fear – use fear to understand the nature of your self.

Sumano Bhikkhu said fear fully entered into his mindfulness practice in the lower cave area one night. "Come over here, I want you to see this," he said. Along the lower chamber's left wall, an aluminum door covered a narrow cave passage only a few feet wide, about six-feet tall and ten-feet deep. He swung open the door. Several crumpled blankets lay on the ground. "The door wasn't always here," he said. "The first year I was here, I slept sitting right there without the door. I found it to be a spot of great concentration. Of course, I was the intruder in this cave. I knew rats sometimes ran through this area to get to a small hole back there. Some bats would fly through, too. I decided I had to get used to them, since I was the new kid on the block."

He said he grew used to the sound of rats scampering through the stone passageway. But one night came a different sound.

"It was pitch black," he said. "I heard what sounded like a female voice in obvious physical distress saying, 'I'm in pain…help me.' This voice was clear as a bell and sounded like it was coming from just a few feet from where I was sitting. But this was impossible since I was down in an inner cave and the upper cave doors were locked! It turned out that I was hearing the voice of a woman trapped under the rubble of a collapsed building 90 miles from here. The next morning, just on intuition, I went to that town and heard about a hotel collapsing. When I met her in the ICU, she sat up immediately, recognizing me. She was cheerful and radiant, even though they had to cut off her legs to free her from the rubble. Sometimes when you meditate with determination and passion, these kinds of phenomena can come up. They make a good story, but they don't advance the struggle for Enlightenment.

"One of the most important things I learned when I began to live alone was the pervasiveness of fear influencing my life," he said. "There is some level, some variety of fear, at play all the time. It can manifest as a well-known fear, such as a fear of physical pain or illness, and then there are the deeply-rooted fears such as spinning into insanity, the fear of loss of dignity, the fear of loss of friendship, the fear of hitting a dead end, the fear of dying before one completes the practice or the fear of an ignominious death – these are some of the fears that become clearer in solitude. "Real solitude offers everyone a taste of what all people seek to know," he said.

Living in the midst of nature, there are also physical dangers that can arouse fear or anxiety in his daily life.

"Poisonous snakes are always around," he said. "The most dangerous time is during the egg laying season when you have to be absolutely attentive to the movements of your body. The main insect menace is mosquitoes. There is almost never a time when one is not attached to some piece of your clothing. Then there are the scorpions and centipedes – many of which are very poisonous. They manage to get into the grot when it rains. They are looking for shelter. You usually get bitten when you feel something running over your body and you instinctively try to push it away in your sleep. They react out of self defense."

Sumano Bhikkhu's life at Double-Eyed Cave is far from the Humboldt Park section of Chicago where he grew up. He boxed in Golden Gloves as a teenager. At age 15, he won the Junior American Bowling award for high school students with a 277 game. He represented his high school on a TV game show designed to showcase outstanding students, "What's the Answer," and placed second, winning a bike and some gift certificates. In the mid 60s he attended college, including three years of law school. He married, began a career in real estate and made a sizeable amount of money, which allowed him to quit work and pursue a spiritual path.

With his wife, he spent two years traveling around the world. When they returned to America, the marriage ended. In his mid-thirties, he began exploring the spiritual supermarket, familiarizing himself with most of the major traditions in the United States, including Judaism, Sufism, Zen Buddhism, Sikhism, Vipassana Buddhism, Hinduism and Tibetan Buddhism. He did all the seminars, life-changing retreats, and martial arts camps that were happening at the time. Finally, he did a three-month meditation retreat.

"I figured that would cook it, and when it was over, I'd d go back to my girlfriend, my motorcycle and my life," he said, "but of course when it was over, I felt all that had pretty much disappeared and that led me to an understanding that I needed a lot more time for myself and that I needed to put a lot more effort into disciplining and developing my mind."

Shortly after that retreat he found himself informally locked into a meditation room on a three-year retreat commitment as he struggled to find direction and meaning in his life.

"That was my first experience with 'house arrest', very useful indeed." he said.

"Rivers and mountains may change human nature never."

Chinese proverb.

The retreat completed, he decided to return to India to find a mature Teacher. However, when his flight passed through London he met a friend who urged him to visit a group of western monks who were just starting a monastery. The monks included Ajahn Sumedho, an Englishman who had studied in Thailand with Ajahn Chaa at the International Meditation Center in a forest east of Ubonratchathani in northeastern Thailand.

"I felt a bonding with Sumedho, and after a week I became close to the group and joined them," he said.

Sumano had lived a comfortable life in California. Life in the English monastery was hard.

"Living in the middle of London in a world of perpetual cold rain was an enormous sacrifice. I secretly hoped that it would pay off!" he said.

He persevered and was the first western monk to be ordained at the monastery. Ajahn Sumano said when he decided to ordain it wasn't because he was depressed, broken-hearted, or incapable of living an ordinary life, unlike some monks he was living with. He said he did feel "heartbroken," but it was "because the world is as it is." He stayed four years in England. But at that time, he said, the training at the monastery was chaotic and emotionally charged- not appropriate for a developing monk. He recognized that he needed a change.

"They wouldn't give me permission to go, so I just packed my things in an old cement sack and waited for something to happen. A few weeks later, an old friend from the high-flying days in Chicago visited me at the monastery. We reminisced about the fast lane lifestyle we shared when we did joint ventures together. Still living the same way he offered me a first-class airline ticket to Thailand but I told him economy would be fine. Actually, I was ready to stand and hold onto a strap the whole way!" Once in Thailand he look up residence in the International Forest Temple east of Ubonratchathani and then at the temple of Ajahn Chaa, near Ubonratchathani, where over a two-year period he was able to spend time and sometimes massage and help nurse Ajahn Chaa, whose health was declining.

"I didn't know what to expect when I came to Thailand," Sumano Bhikkhu said, recalling his early days in the country. "It certainly wasn't anything like I thought it would be. It was much harder. It was just about over the top. You're coming to a new place, you're 45 years old, you don't know the food, the language, the culture. It's so bloody hot. And now I'm suddenly eating lizard stew, roasted ants, and other exotic dishes. But I had made a commitment that I was going to stick to it. I don't know that I would have gone into it if I'd known how hard it was going to be."

Geckos which are small, spongy lizards, are a common protein foods in the poor, rural Thais also included roasted beetles and other insects.

"People would see me coming on my alms round," he said, "and grab a stick, reach up into a tree to catch a beetle and bring it to the frying pan in one swift motion. Often, I had roasted beetle, rice and a banana for my meal. I had to make a decision. Which would be dessert? Also, in the Issan villages (Eastern Thailand), the curry peppers are fiery hot. If you blow on those peppers they ignite immediately. The peppers were usually chopped up and might be the main ingredient in many of my meals. All the farangs (Westerners) would try to eat around them, but few succeeded"

Sharing the same food of the people you live among was one of the first rules established by the Buddha, and is now one of the 227 Rules of Conduct for *thudong* monks. The rules allow a monk to walk through the community for morning alms, and to eat one meal a day before noon. "Alms round is generally misunderstood," Sumano Bhikkhu said. "The common Thai definition is, 'Begging for food,' but in reality it's the creation of an opportunity for people to make an offering, to make a sacrifice. That's where *boon*, or good merit, or *karma*, comes in. If there's no sacrifice, there's no *boon*. A rich person can give something, but unless there's a sacrifice they're not really getting merit. The idea of sacrifice is one of the keys to all religions."

Before the Buddha, he said, many sadhus, or religious aspirants in India, used to seek alms by holding out their hands while standing in front of a dwelling. Sometimes a *sadhu* would hold out a hollow skull they might have found in a charnel ground.

"That was one of the reasons the Buddha allowed monks to carry bowls for alms," Sumano Bikkhu said. Pointing to his own polished steel alms bowl, he said, "That's the Rolls Royce of bowls. Before steel bowls, they were usually ceramic. If you dropped the bowl and it broke, you might not eat for several days while you were pasting it back together. The Buddha set up the alms round so monks would interact with common people. Monk would have to have the respect of the people, or they wouldn't be given food."

The training of *Thudong* monks is centered in meditation or mindfulness practice, known as Vipassana or insight practice. A typical meditation schedule for a *thudong* monk during intensive practice is as follows:

3:00 a.m.	rise, bathe, practice light yoga
3:30 a.m.	chanting
4:00 a.m.	fast walking meditation, 15 mins; slow walking, 30 mins.
4:45 a.m.	itting meditation until first light.
First light	house chores followed by alms rounds, up to 7 km
7:00 a.m.	sitting meditation
7:30 a.m.	correspondence, writing projects.
8:30 a.m.	eat
10:00-11:00 a.m.	walking and sitting meditation.
11:00 a.m.	rest period
12:00-1:00 p.m.	sleep
1:00-5:00 p.m.	sitting and walking meditation.
5:00 p.m.	rest, hot drink.
5:30 p.m.	water plants, bathe.
7:00 p.m – midnight	walking and sitting meditation

When in intensive meditation practice, a person can get by with three to four hours of sleep a night, because of the long periods of meditation. Sumano Bhikku said he tries to go from sitting meditation to sleep in a seamless transition. "This is critical to maintain a lighter sleep instead of a heavy sleep, where you're 'out of it,'" he said. "You wake up feeling brighter and thinking, 'I need every minute of this day to do the day's activities.'"

Only a few *thudong* masters, then in their 70s and 80s, were alive when Sumano Bhikkhu arrived in Thailand. But the *Thudong* lineage in Thailand is still strong and is still practiced today secluded, generally isolated areas. "I got a big taste of the tradition," Sumano Bhikkhu said. "The most vigorous *thudong* pathway today is in the lineage of Ajahn Chaa. It is still going on and has an impeccable reputation for its deep-rooted training. Young monks still practice *thudong* way, aspiring to recognize each action of the body and mind. Simplicity is the key.

He eventually moved on from the International Meditation Center and undertook solitary practice while traveling in Asia. "I didn't come to Thailand with the idea that I was going to walk around Asia. I did enough, though. I did a penniless walkabout through India for eight months.

While the *thudong* monks of the past wandered throughout Thailand, often crossing into Burma and Laos, such free access to vast wilderness areas is impossible today. A few remaining Thai forests are found only in national parks. The government officially prohibits monks from living in the park areas. Critics say it is to prevent monks from observing and reporting illegal tree cutting.

During the early half of the 20th century, the *thudong* tradition underwent a "revivalist" period. In those early days, *thudong* practice was grueling and hard as steel, designed for the very few monks who had the physical and mental strength to commit their lives to extreme physical renunciation. *Thudong* monks are still prohibited from engaging in activities that do not call for sharing or teaching of the dharma. The sparsely written records of the *Thudong* masters is noticeably void of the soft palliative language often found in contemporary Buddhist writing, in both the East and the West. The unrelenting reality of daily mindfulness practice within a lifestyle of extreme isolation and deprivation was the fundamental practice ground for *Thudong* monks who saw themselves as struggling against the unwholesome forces found inside the mind and within all cultures. In Sanskrit, such unwholesome forces are called kilesa (defilements). For *thudong* monk, feeling of fear and suffering were seen to be no different than feeling of vanity, greed or pride. They were simply state of mind, which all people feel and which might be profitably exploited and eventually overcome.

Nearest to all things is that power that fashions their being.

Henry David Thoreau

The *Thudong* master credited with bringing the lineage to full flower is Ajahn Mun (circa 1871 to 1949). He left behind a dozen disciple monks who were eventually recognized as *thudong* masters themselves. They in turn left behind many disciples who are still practicing today in Thailand and around the world, though perhaps not in as rigorous a manner. Under Ajahn Mun, a monk's early training was spent at his teacher's side. The novice received oral instruction and also learned by observing. After higher levels of training were absorbed, novices would be sent off to practice on their own or in the company of a few fellow monks or novices. I was expected that they would continue to deepen their practice in solitude and to consult with their teacher whenever needed, but especially during the annual rains retreat. These yearly, intense practice sessions during July through September are based on one of the 227 rules handed down by the Buddha.

"Do not look for the dharma outside yourself," Ajahn Mun always advised his disciples. "The dharma is neither in palm-leaf books nor in a monastery. A monastery is merely a place where monks reside. Neither is dharma in the air or in the forest. The dharma is within ourselves."

He always said nature was his true teacher: plants, weather and animals, the way of Nature.

"After ordination my Ajahn took me wandering in the forests and on the mountains," Mun said. "I learned the dharma from the trees, the grass, rivers, streams, and the distractions that arise from material accumulations. For Nietzsche, the ascetic ideal offers a protective path, a way to preserve a spiritual calling, to defend it from the predictable spiritual deterioration that commonly occurs when an aspirant is surrounded by the forces of everyday culture. Practicing any extreme form of ascetic deprivation, Nietzsche believed, arises from an individual's desire for transformation, or "rebirth," in the process of "willing," or entailing a movement toward "a will to nothingness, a revulsion from [normal] life." But for Nietzsche – and for *thudong* monks – the use of deprivation and hardship, staples on the ascetic road, is only a technique to reach a far different and ultimate gold – the fullness of being human. As a simple trope, Nietzsche said the ascetic ideal signifies "the wish to be different, to be elsewhere." It signifies a reflection of disappointment with the world *as it is*, or appears to be, for the bulk of humanity. In Dawn of Day, aphorism 119, he struck at the core of the matter for *thudong* monks, declaring, "All our so-called consciousness is a more or less fantastic commentary upon an unknown text, one that is perhaps unknowable but still felt."

Sumano Bhikkhu counts himself lucky to have known Ajahn Chaa and Ajahn Tate, two disciples of Ajahn Mun who later became master teachers. "Ajahn Chaa didn't have a lot of energy left," he said. "He couldn't speak, and he had limited movement, but his eyes and brain were fully functional and capable of piercing into your heart." Sumano Bhikkhu attended to both Ajahn Chaa and Ajahn Tate on different occasions, giving foot massages to Ajahn Chaa, who lost his mobility near the end of his life.

"In the past, a lot of teachers were available, but they left no records," he said. "Ajahn Chaa was western-oriented. He liked tape recorders. He had a sense of the enduring value of the voice of Truth. He understood that any dharma talk was a manifestation of a teacher's whole life. He would pull a tape recorder right up in front of him to be sure it captured his words."

The importance of leaving a record probably explains Sumano Bhikkhu's interest in writing and his acceptance of computers – leaving his own record. A disciple donated an old Mac laptop, knowing Sumano Bhikkhu had stacks of scribbled notes, journals and diaries. Sumano Bhikkhu worked on writing projects on the laptop in 45-minute bursts, and then recharged the battery. Since the publication of "Questions From The City, Answers From The Forest" and "Meeting The Monkey Half Way," he regularly receives e-mails and letters from around the world. It amuses him that if a person orders one of his books from Amazon.com, they automatically are offered a suggestion that they might also like a book by Ajahn Chaa. "That's electronic karmic connection," he said.

Sumano Bhikkhu has translated numerous talks by the master *thudong* monks. He has also published a self-printed, free book, The Brightened Mind aimed at teaching children the art of concentration, which can help them maintain interest in the classroom and excel in their studies.

By Sumano Bhikkhu's estimate, there might be two hundred *thudong* monks of high attainment today in Thailand. "About one in five are really able to do it," he said, "but the other four are quite okay. It's a noble lifestyle. If you can perfect it, you reach impeccability, providing you with the techniques and skills to stabilize the mind in the present moment, where incisive wisdom emerges. If you get all that together, you have a "supermonk." in Thailand. "If you were an astute young monk or lay person, you would want to spend some time with these monks."

Looking back on his 25 years of practice, Sumano Bhikkhu said he now appreciates more fully the Buddha's meaning of suffering. "What I have learned is that there is a lot of physical, psychological and emotional suffering in all our lives," he said. "Using that, you can clear out a lot of the internal, hardwired part of the mental rubbish. In fact, the intensity of suffering is the great teacher. In *thudong* practice, you're clearly pushed and locked into challenging situations. You're totally handicapped by the 227 rules of the order. You don't have any money; you eat once a day, you can't talk to women alone. You can only go through your memory files for so long. It creates a 'hot house' for practice, something a person can't escape from. Ultimately, practice is the striving to come to that pure perspective that allows the present moment to be seen and penetrated."

Thudong monks practice Vipassana or insight meditation, which is based on constant attention to the movement of the mind and body. Daily life is the practice ground of mindfulness. Attention to the mind's movement is usually contrasted with concentration meditation, or meditation as traditionally practiced in Zen Buddhism, which commonly focuses the mind on a single object, usually the movement of breath, a word or a phrase. Actually, both approaches to meditation traditionally use both mindfulness and concentration meditation, but insight meditation pushes a person more quickly into the deep water of paying attention to the moment-to-moment movement of the body and mind.

In Vipassana practice, all thoughts, sensations or physical movements are seen as based on mental or sensory attachments or processes, to internal conceptions or external objects, "But there's much more to be learned about the workings of the mind," Sumano Bhikkhu said.

"Because there is dissolution and reformation of mental thoughts and sensations, there must necessarily be empty or free space. Space exists on either side of a micro-moment of consciousness formation [in the mind] as it comes into being and dissolves again. So there is actually twice as much space as there is formation. Here is a quantitative expression of the reality of emptiness. In conventional life, we emphasize the formation phase, the micro-moments that create a field of tremendous, unstoppable activity. In dharma training, we emphasize the space before and after, which is the more prevalent reality by at least two to one."

"You use the 227 rules of conduct, which are a technique, and you try to let go of everything else, including the dharma and everything you've come to consider yourself to be. Somewhere at the bottom of that extremely hard process is a space where people can meet their true nature and gain wisdom."

The ancient rules of conduct advise monks to seek out isolated places for their practice including cemeteries or charnel grounds. For several years, Sumano Bhikkhu practiced in the modern equivalent to a charnel ground by hitchhiking rides to a forensic hospital in Bangkok where he was allowed to observe autopsies. He stood by the side of a highway, wearing a sign pinned to his robe reading: "I'm practicing silence."

"It's really the only kind of cemetery practice you can do today," he said. "The point is to recover balance. Death needs to become real. We have been conditioned to venerate birth and to blot out death." During and after observing autopsies, he experienced intense mental sensations and images. "It could be something like a hand or teeth or an internal organ of the body. I would come back and work with these images of the body in relation to death. I worked on this practice for years. Our bodies have all kinds of stinky parts. We're falling apart and disintegrating – we're on our way to death. From the time you're in the womb of your mother to when you come out, you're on your way to death. If all you get in life is input about the beauty and sensuality of the body, you end up with a distorted view. It's a sobering practice."

As he told the story, I recalled a sentence printed at the bottom of each of his e-mails: "The deception of death is the big lie...the rest follow."

As the evening shadows deepened at the Double-Eyed Cave compound, a local Thai farmer with his wife and child walked through the gate, part of a stream of visitors and disciples who visit on weekends. Visitors are now a part of Sumano Bhikkhu's practice at the cave retreat. He answers questions and offers guidance through the dharma knowing it's where his karma has taken him. But he remains rooted in his practice.

"All of this, everything could change quickly,- nothing is permanent," he said, looking off toward the mountain. And with that, he picked up a broom and continued to sweep leaves.

24 Monk in the mountain

Preface

The questions in this book came from transcriptions and notes extracted from dialogues here at this retreat sanctuary. As this is a personal retreat meditation place, we aren't listed in any Buddhist directories nor do we encourage visitors. No courses are offered and visiting hours are restricted. The sign in front of the road is just about big enough to make out the words "Double Eyed Cave". Most people who have never visited here miss it on their first try. We do what we can to try and protect the silence and solitude through anonymity. However, the website (www.next-life.com) is monitored and we make an attempt to respond to people's queries via the net.

This is the second book of this type published. The earlier one, titled "Questions from the City, Answers from the Forest" sold out and is no longer available. We will publish this book ourselves and see that it is distributed throughout Asia for as long as the passionate interest in contemplating "the-way-things-are" continues to grow. That earlier book dealt with questions from hikers who visited the national park adjacent to these caves. Most spoke of their anxiety and distress concerning the environment, their governments, jobs, and the workplace. These young people felt angry and alienated from the contempt, arrogance and corruption that is causing so much suffering in the world, especially concerning the unabated and rampant destruction of our ecosystem. There are more skillful ways to relate to nature, other people, and other cultures. This book points the way.

Now, in the 21st century, we focused on questions concerning karma, dealing with separation and death, terrorism, how to find happiness, and developing the mind within the everyday world. Seemingly, there is a conflict in trying to integrate spiritual practices into the chaos of the everyday world. There isn't…you will come to understand that what we have is what we need and that there is no dilemma here. The questions posed came from a wide spectrum of guests. Their ages ranged from 18 to 75 and their countries as diverse as Australia and Zimbabwe.

Many, many friends helped put this together for you. Luang Por Punnyananda Bhikkhu, Yom Gaan Punyaratabandhu advisor, Yom Neung producer, Yom Bubby editor, Yom On photographer, Yom Ut and Mam graphic designers, Yom Roy Hamric and Yom Teddy proofreading, Yom Kosol, Gnahmpis, and Winnie Wongsurawat, Yom Keith and Wantanee bell, Yom Sam, Porn, and Nalisa Sitabut, Yom Punjaphorn and Benz, Yom Suraphan, Yom Sayan-Oy, Dr. Jutaraht, Yom Jin, Fred Weick, Dr. Kumaratankuma, Yom Anjalee, Yom Kusama, Yom Orathai, Yom Jahr and Pomphet, the Thai-Danish Milk Cooperative, and many, many others, all supported this project in various ways.

If you realize that all things change,
there is nothing you will try to hold on to.
If you aren't afraid of dying,
there is nothing you can't achieve.

If you want to shrink something, you must first allow it to expand.
If you want to get rid of something, you must first allow it to flourish.
If you want to take something, you must first allow it to be given.
This is called the subtle perception of the way things are.

The soft overcomes the hard.
The slow overcomes the fast.
Let your workings remain a mystery;
Just show people the results.

True words aren't eloquent;
Eloquent words aren't true.
Wise men don't need to prove their point;
Men who need to prove their point aren't wise.

If you look to others for fulfillment,

You will never truly be fulfilled.
If your happiness depends on money,
You will never be happy with yourself.

Be content with what you have;
Rejoice in the way things are.
When you realize there is nothing lacking,
The whole world belongs to you.

"The-Way-Things-Are"

This book is dedicated to the Thai people in every country who support the offering of the Buddha's Teachings. May you all be happy,

live long, and be at peace.

Ajahn Sumano Bhikkhu

Q. **When I feel happy, am I free of suffering?**

A. The suffering is in the *looking* for happiness. When you are content, there is no searching; your mind rests in its original abiding. Is that true? See for yourself.

Q. **If everything changes, why bother?**

A. Through bothering, you come to understand the fact of change and then, nothing can bother you.

Q. **In meditation, sometimes my mind goes back to an earlier memory and sees things from a wider, more beneficial aspect than I ever recollected before. Would you consider this a useful aspect of meditation?**

A. When you sit down and close your eyes to practice meditation, all kinds of memories, fantasies, melodramas, and action-thrillers will arise. Actually, the mind has no shame...anything can pop up into it. Occasionally, some things will come together in a way that sheds light on a previously hidden aspect of a past event. Sometimes you will remember the drawer where you put a bill or claim check. You have restrained input by closing your eyes so the mind has room to catch up on the everyday matters that have not been cleared. For that reason alone, sitting quietly is beneficial. However, meditation isn't about catching up, it's about clearing, purifying and energizing. In a fundamental way, authentic meditation only occurs when you are present. Everything off the present moment is irrelevant. Meditation is an activity that occurs in a dimension beyond the conventional world. Don't think this as being too far off and inaccessible. It is something you can do and its value is far greater than the effort it requires.

Q. **If you say that the present is all there is and the past and future are illusions, how can I plan for my future?**

A. The future is an illusion in relation to absolute reality which is only the present. Still, as long as the past and future have such power over you and you still believe in them, then you will worry about your future and try to make it better, safer than the past. You will build your future out of your past and the effect will be more of the same. Your future is waiting for you along the time continuum. Unless there is the insertion of wisdom, you will repeat the past. No matter how much you might fret and worry about the future, things will remain relatively the same. Why? Because worry, proliferation, and seeking answers only from past experiences will merely create another variety of the past. Radical, creative thought emerges out of the present from touching the timelessness in meditation. This energy is employable and is effective in every situation---as long as you allow it to meet the future. That's because the present is comprehensive, aware of the past but not dominated by it, radical in a creative sense, and, ultimately, fearless.

Q. **How big a part does experience play in the potency of wisdom?**

A. Truth comes from experience and intuition. Wisdom brings perspective. With a wise perspective on life we focus on what is important and avoid what is toxic. So, at the fundamental level, experience can be an important guide. Later, experience can be a burden as it prevents us from seeing things with fresh eyes and an empty mind.

Q. **How do you look at the terrorism that is generating so much fear in the world today?**

A. To me, terrorism and exploitation are the same energies. Both spring from greed and lack of compassion. Both target the innocent and vulnerable. Both manifest selfishness and cowardice. In all societies, the exploitation of women, labor, children, and the poor has long been widespread to become the convention. Terrorism is intimately affiliated with this energy.

Vile and pitiless terrorism epitomizes the amalgamation of all the evil energies in the world. It operates solely with the intention to harm and kill and has no compunctions about maiming innocent children, the defenseless, or the harmless. It is shameless, abhors kindness and scorns compassion. From what I understand, proponents of terrorism are often enslaved into a simplistic political ideology functioning on the notion that evil brings good both in this world and the next. It is senseless and outrageous and goes against the basis of all religions. When people blindly believe in others, it takes very little effort to brainwash them into doing anything for any reason whatsoever.

Q. **I still don't get why you regard doubt as insidious. When doubt comes in and disturbs me, I am forced to consider the situation in a deeper way. Doubt forces me to investigate before I make my move.**

A. That's putting quite a positive spin on a pernicious problem. Doubt short-circuits psychological energy. You haven't been noticing the suffering that arrives with the doubt. It casts us into hesitation and hesitation is the result of confusion. When we are caught in doubt we are helpless. When you come to a decision, it doesn't necessarily mean that doubt is gone. Often we are *still* under the power of doubt even after we manage to make a decision. Unless that decision is iron-clad, utterly decisive, doubt has us reconsidering our choice.

The far superior alternative is spontaneous choice. This occurs only under the power of Wisdom. Wisdom rather than thought decides so that whatever decision arises, that decision marks the end of the quandary. Because wisdom was involved in the decision making process, there was no stress, no suffering. After deciding the mind is free to move on without backtracking or second-guessing.

Q. I am a career soldier. I have always wanted to be a soldier in order to serve my Queen and my country. In the military academy we are taught that the profession of a soldier is the highest profession because we are the people who offer our lives in service in order to defend our country and conquer our enemies.

You were just saying that you thought being a monk is the ultimate way to live a life. I am curious to know why you think that way. I just see you as a good person helping people with the problems in their lives.

A.   My life is dedicated to conquering myself. That may not sound like much until you've tried it. It is the toughest, most exhausting enterprise anyone can take on. Even if you understand what this pursuit demands---the annihilation of all illusion---you still might not regard it as all that significant. Even if you recognize the nobility of the quest, you may think that, regardless of whether one succeeds or not, it just a matter of one person arriving at a point where he/she sees the world clearly and can no longer be fooled by anything whatsoever. Actually, it is nothing less than the transformation of one ordinary person into a distinguished human being. That person is Enlightened. He/she becomes a living Light for everyone. The point I am making is that there is far more to this journey than meets the eye.

Q.   **I am in a quandary concerning money. There is a lot of advertising out in the real world that encourages me to go out and make a pile. In my circle of friends this has become, after years at university, the primary objective in our lives. I am having trouble with this because the generally accepted notion is that once I attain this wealth that they say I am entitled to, I will be happy, no longer lonely and can finally enjoy my life. Somehow that doesn't ring true. And yet it doesn't ring false either!**

A.   As with all intimate relationships, money demands that you be aware of what you are doing and what you're involved in. This means that you have to look at your relationship to money with circumspection and from several dimensions. Endeavor to recognize that all money isn't the same. Some money brings harm to the owner. Much depends on how it was accumulated and whom it came from. Money is a heavy karmic entity. How many hands does money pass through before wearing out? Have there been times when the money came by way of exploiting some person or animal? When you see the situation with circumspection and discrimination, you will certainly know that you won't find much happiness by striving to get your "pile" at any cost and by any means.

The fundamental principle concerning Happiness is that it can only be tasted in the here and now. If you have to do something, if you have to create the conditions for your Happiness, you will never really come to it.

Q. **Strict Buddhists believe that one shouldn't drink alcohol. I don't drink a lot nor do I drink often. I don't see the harm in moderation.**

A. Allow me to answer that concern in as straightforward manner as I can. Alcohol is an age-old trap. Do you think dulling your mind improves your life? The only time it can be of benefit to anybody is in a ritual. And, in that context one has to see that it is a means to an end, a point of focus. It can be useful in helping to bond people together, and to bring concord to the moment. As with any stimulant, we have to recognize the need to control it. Control comes out of discipline and discipline comes out of wisdom. I am talking about a discipline of love, not a discipline enforced by fear. We must have the power to control rather than be controlled or else we carry on oblivious to our slavery. Also, alcohol, according to scientists, acts as both a depressant and a stimulant. Why would anyone want to be under the influence of these conflicting energies?

Q.   **The more I read about Buddhism the more curious and interested I become. I am interested in learning more about this subject.**

A.   What you have come upon is not just interesting, it is profound. This is an important distinction.

Within the profound there is an extraordinary world waiting to be discovered. One must study spirituality from the right starting point, the right attitude.

Be careful that you aren't pursuing your interest in Buddhism just to become a more interesting person, a dabbler who knows some word bytes about some fashionable topic.

Buddhism offers us the opportunity to see things in a deeper way. Actually, learning about our spiritual nature won't make us more interesting, it will make us *less* interesting.

No doubt you will find that an interesting thought!

Q. What are the symptoms of the state of mindfulness?

A. Mindfulness-Awareness is called "Sati" in the Pali language . In English we can call it "Love", Spiritual Love. It is the state of being fully in the moment, fully awake, and fully responsive. If that's not Love, what other state of being or experience is worthy of being called Love?

What else can anyone say about a state of being that can only be known by its flavor?

Q. Is paranoia a spiritual problem?

A. Definitely. Paranoia is like a magician who has the skill and cunning to place all kinds of pieces of things, bits of this and that, into one mental construct. That which is constructed can be precisely what you have come to fear the most. It is quite an amazing manifestation. This is not something that only crazy people encounter. It is very much part of human experience. We all need to develop the strength of mind to see through the tricks the mind plays, so as not to get entangled in anything that pops up in it. It's only a weak mind that creates the opportunity for paranoia to overwhelm and overpower the mind.

Q. My parents hammered into me with the belief that they were always right. By the time I graduated college and went to work, I felt like my opinion on anything and everything was valueless. It took me many years to feel some confidence about my beliefs. And, now, after practicing meditation for some months I can see that ALL beliefs have no actual roots, have no basis in fact.

A. In a short time you already developed an undistorted perspective on your life. People who have done a lot of good and a lot of investigation in the past develop quickly. So, now you have an intelligent standpoint from which to observe the true nature of belief and opinion. Belief is just belief. Opinion is just opinion. I always smile when I read about the results of some so-called "opinion poll". What makes opinion worth anything? As a matter of fact, people are always right from where they are coming from. They are correct from the point of their bias, their lack of understanding, their ignorance, and their limitations. This is certainly far removed from Truth. With wisdom, there is no one point from which anything issues forth.

At the root of all the animosities that arise between different tribes, different cultures lies hidden their firmly established sense of righteousness. That is, simply stated, their unsubstantiated belief system. Belief that is unrelated to Truth.

From the perspective of Buddha-Dhamma, we see that people who are tenaciously stuck in their opinions suffer from an identity crisis. It's a different kind of identify crisis than we normally think of. If they stopped identifying with their tribe and their culture, they could accommodate and live in harmony with others. If we see the world from fact, we would see that all beings are brothers and sisters in aging, illness and death. That's not belief; that's Truth.

Q. Sometimes when difficult situations arise I am presented with various choices that all seem equally good. How do I choose which is best?

A. Just do what is appropriate.

Q. How do I know what's appropriate?

A. You won't know...but wisdom will.

Q. I have three small children to look after. They demand all my time and energy. I see them as my practice.

A. They are certainly going to be a challenge to your ability to cope but that's not the same as engaging your life in practice. The practice is where everything that you acknowledge, be it feelings, memory, etc., reflects off of your inner refuge which all spiritual practitioners call mindfulness. You certainly can use this difficult situation for practice. You need only be cognizant of the observer. Without the observer, you are only "mother". With the observer, you are "mother minding children and minding mother with circumspect awareness."

Q. I think I understand the problems that come with a mind beset by doubt. What I would like to know about involves some kind of intelligence required even before I reach the doubting stage. That is, what criteria should be used in determining which choices should be put up for consideration? A few minutes ago you used the example of choosing ice cream flavors. These days there are dozens of choices. Before limiting my choices to two or three, what is it that brings a particular flavor to the forefront?

In my daily life I might have to choose between several jobs, several politicians, and several places to live. You see what I am getting at?

A. What you're asking isn't all that different from the vanilla-chocolate analogy I often hold up as testimony to the way we tend to operate. The decisions you are talking about tend to come out of one's past experience. Before I liked something, so today I will go after the same thing. This repetition indicates how little choice people have as they lead their lives down familiar tracks.

As a monk, I am much more concerned with how to live a wise and holy life. Obviously, we have many mundane decisions to make everyday. And we should endeavor to make good decisions. However, I am concerned more with the decisions that have profound meaning. What I see as praiseworthy are decisions that call for accepting personal pain and considerable sacrifice. Decisions that go against one's self interest because *it is the right thing to do.* When the decisions involve loyalty to country, to religious faith, to a political ideal or social cause, those who go against the powerful instinct for self- preservation in order to support something greater than their own personal well being I regard as noble. People who live and act in this way are people with integrity, with dignity, and with power. Many themes in popular movies and plays dramatize people who act with courage and nobility. The main element that they dramatize is that heroic beings act unselfishly, regardless of what the personal cost to them might be. The choices they decide upon have nothing whatsoever to do with secure or agreeable memories or with conventional happiness. They do what's right and appropriate in a particular moment. In Buddhism, we call this "meeting the moment with wisdom and compassion". We all have the possibility of meeting every moment with wisdom and compassion. All that needs to be done is to subdue the notion of who we think we are and stop following negative emotions. If we accomplish this feat, we will have done the most heroic thing that can be achieved in this lifetime.

Q. **There is someone I live with in a communal home who tends to continually mess things up. I have often tried to tell her how to deal with some of the problems that arise in our living space but she just goes on her merry, sloppy, clumsy way. Are there some people who are unable to change their lives for the better?**

A. There are people who are untrainable. I doubt that your housemate is in that unfortunate category. I suspect that she just isn't ready to learn. She may not be open to learning from certain people, people with certain conflicting personalities. In this case, you may just not be the right person to teach. If that's the case, you don't have the authority to offer her your suggestions. Or maybe, the timing is wrong. Timing is a critical factor in this kind of dynamic. Sometimes the situation is clogged with emotions or karma. So the situation needs to be right also.

We have to depend upon whatever wisdom we can utilize. And, as I mentioned a moment ago, her mind could be too thick, too dense to learn anything from anybody regardless of these other factors.

You're not alone. I am always seeing people do foolish things here in the Wat but if I feel they are not ready to learn, I've learned that the appropriate response is to just observe and wish them well. Interestingly, there have been a few times I thought someone was doing something in an awkward fashion that turned out in the end to be more effective than the suggestion I had in mind.

Q. **I can see that this passing show, called life, presents us with a whole spectrum of events and situations. Some I have enjoyed while some I have hated. The ones that I had trouble enduring seemed to go on forever. In retrospect, I have to say that I don't do well when faced with devastating difficulty. When the worst possible scenarios occur, where is the best place to take one's stance?**

A. You can do as I do, endeavor to see everything that happens in life as events presented for my benefit and, ultimately, for the benefit of all sentient beings. Therefore, whatever happens, no matter how difficult, I regard as positive and as events which are endurable.

I haven't always faced life in this way. In the early years of my meditation practice perplexing and weird memories mixed with blazing emotions occurred out of nowhere which tied me up mentally and emotionally. Now I can see that they were, for the most part, unresolved passions from previous lifetimes. I felt paralyzed and in that state felt vulnerable, helpless, and even hopeless. All throughout the recovery time I felt lost, disappointed, angry, and bewildered. Those kind of heavy situations take time to be processed. We have to endure, absorb, and contemplate, before they can finally be understood and left behind. See that things will ultimately provide you with the opportunity to develop wisdom, and that everything that arises must pass away.

Q. **Why meditate? I like to put on make-up and party.**

A. O.K. Then see it as beauty parlor service that will help take the wrinkles out of your mind. I can understand your attitude towards meditation. For once we have settled down in our habitual ways of living and thinking, we feel less and less inclined to give them up for the sake of risky ventures. Maybe you should wait on meditation for a while.

Q. **Some time ago, through a series of very strange misunderstandings, I was humiliated by a group of people who I thought were my friends. You know, those 5 minutes dominate all other memories in my mind. It was such a powerfully painful experience involving a sense of betrayal, disappointment, anger, frustration, etc. that it has come to be the "revert" in my mind. By "revert" I mean the place where my mind goes back to when it is not actively involved in anything.**

A. I too had a similar humiliating experience. It took some time to get perspective on it, but when I did I realized that I could endure that kind of attack on my ego because I am not my ego. "Sticks and stones can break my bones but words can never hurt me".

This is a folk maxim that carries considerable Truth. A scenario of humiliation provokes strong reaction because we believe we are who we think we are. We are not. See it that way, and that will be the end of the story.

Q. **I have always been a fearful person. I guess I was born that way. Other kids would see adventure; I would back away out of fear. Even my youngest sister would call me a "scaredy cat". I know that fear has forced me to choose a safe job, an apartment in a building with high security, and friends who are very much like me. Still, I feel fearful at work and in my apartment. If you are born afraid, is it one's destiny to die terrified? That's my biggest fear.**

A. Anxiety is useful in that it alerts us to danger. We have this fragile body and there are many ways to injure ourselves. Anxiety sends out a warning signal: it's dark or slippery, watch your step; this is an electrical appliance---be careful; this is a dangerous intersection---slow down, etc. However, when anxiety oversteps its proper boundaries, fear arises. Once fear arises, it can take over and drive us crazy. We can become terrified of everything. It can dis-empower us. Obviously, we need to marshal anxiety to warn us of dangers but not allow anxiety to morph into full-blown fear.

You were not born with any more fear than anyone else. You allowed fear to dominate and manipulate you. You can re-establish the right relationship between anxiety and reality. Also, nobody has a "destiny" to live and die consumed by fear. That's ridiculous. If you are willing to make the effort to energize your mind through meditation, your fears will slither away and you will die in peace.

Q. Can I ask you a question concerning loneliness? I don't understand why the feeling of loneliness disturbs me so much or why it even comes about. When it comes on, it just comes out of the blue. I believe myself to be quite independent, self-sufficient and intelligent. When I am alone, I enjoy the aloneness. Or, I use the solitude to read and write. I am capable of engaging in many activities that bring me satisfaction and a sense of personal development. I don't understand why I should feel lonely when there is no particular determinant that kicks it off.

A. It's likely that you are experiencing existential loneliness. This is the feeling of loneliness that cannot be cured by the company of others or even the fascination of something new and engaging. It comes and goes on its own: sitting in an airport lounge, pouring a drink at a party, standing in an elevator with a half dozen other passengers.

The determining factor, regardless of whether or not you catch it, is the recognition that we are alone. We are born alone and we die alone. And nothing can drown out that fact. Instead of being puzzled or bewildered about that feeling, contemplate it. Its arising has given you the opportunity to turn your attention to "the-way-things-are".

Q.   How can I make better choices?

A.   Life is chock full of choices so your question is clearly relevant
to all our lives. The quality of your life depends on the quality
of your choices. And the quality of choices depends upon the
evolution of your wisdom. Wisdom is circumspect awareness.
If you want to make better choices, more appropriate decisions,
meditate. Your mind will strengthen. You will nourish your
mind by being present and aware. When we are not being
present and are unaware, our thoughts tend to orbit around
plans to fulfill our desires, which are endless, or strategies to
allay our hidden fears, and that kind of neurotic proliferation is
also endless. When fear and desire dominate our thoughts, they
will also dominate our choices. We make better choices when
the mind is under our control and observed with the awareness
faculty which is built into our minds.

**Q.   What is "kilesa"? I have come upon this word many times
recently.**

A.   They are the dark influences, the dark and dense influences
which contaminate the original, pure mind. They are the things
which precipitate suffering. The most difficult ones are: desire,
anger, and ignorance. These energies pollute and corrupt our
ability to see things and accept things as they are. Associated with
these three corrupting energies are: hope (because it projects us
into the future), greed (because it generates selfishness), jealousy
(because it won't accept the good fortune that has come to
another being), and impatience (because it won't allow events to
take their natural course). Our meditation practice is designed
to overcome these kinds of pollutants.

The critical causal factor is ignorance. Ignorance is so pervasive and so familiar that some have said that seeing it for what it is, is like "looking at the back of one's eyes".

Q.   **I am here today because I can see that the things I do in my life don't give me much satisfaction. Like the rock singer said, "I don't get no satisfaction". I know I am young and that young people are supposed to run around and have fun. I have done a lot of running around, but I rarely had fun. And the fun I had ended up causing pain for myself or others. I am hoping you can tell me what I can do to feel better about myself.**

A.   I don't know what kind of activities you got caught up in which dishonored your life and wasted a piece of your life but I suspect they involved a lot of desire and self indulgence. To waste one's youth in foolishness is hardly uncommon. In that regard, you are quite normal. From another vantage point, you are quite exceptional. You want to live and act in a way that has deeper purpose.

The key to what you seek is to incline your life towards activities that connect to your Heart, rather than your body or even your mind. If you look carefully at your life, you will see that the ability to garner long-lasting satisfaction from things that are essentially empty is hopeless. (Just as trying to find happiness from things and activities that you don't really need.) Push your life forward onto a plateau where your lifestyle is moderate, simple, and green. You will find that by working for only that which you need---food, clothing, shelter and medicine, your life automatically becomes more satisfying. The amount of disappointment and doubt you normally experience will reduce dramatically. The intelligent things you desire can be obtained in a straight-forward manner. You won't be harboring excessive or extravagant desires. You can find real Happiness with little. And you will increase your Happiness exponentially through reducing selfishness and increasing selflessness.

If you live in this way, continuously inclining your life towards Heart-connected meaning, when it comes time to die, you will die peacefully and without regret.

Q. **I can't put the Buddha's Teaching in context with "I think therefore I am". From that statement it seems that thinking is the thing which distinguishes us as a human being. Yet, the meditation you teach is aimed at subduing and controlling thought.**

A. Better to have said, "Observing thought therefore I am". When you observe thought, what is it that observes? Isn't it some kind of energy with the power to control, investigate, and penetrate? Thought is merely a stream of mind bytes producing images and feeling from whatever happens to be in our consciousness. These are then delivered to awareness. When there is no control over this mind stuff, whatever arises is absorbed directly into consciousness. When this machine-like action takes place we have no control, no perspective on that which impacted upon awareness. You have nothing, no leverage, to observe and evaluate thought. If thoughts weren't insidious, that would be no problem. But thought is random, it is boundary-less, and shameless. It is a machine that isn't working for our highest interests.

Contemplate what I just said and you will recognize that there is far more freedom from within a discipline of observation than from casually following and acting on errant thoughts.

Q. I spent a few decades trying to figure what was what in this world. I used to hang around in a gang in my neighborhood because feeling part of a group seemed very important to me. Later, I had a chance to go to college. Being a student became my identity. After graduation I got a good job in a company. My work then seemed to be the most important thing in my life. For a while I felt satisfied with my life. However, after two years the job just became tedious and shallow. Actually, any sense of satisfaction also evaporated, just as it did when I was a gang member, and a student. Now, I have been traveling around the world for almost three years looking for something or other. I don't know what I'm looking for, but I do know I haven't found it yet.

A. What you're searching for is meaning in your life. It sounds like you got a little taste of it as you made your way through life. Just getting a little taste here and there has been enough for you to recognize the importance of meaning but not enough to satisfy your hunger. Consciously or unconsciously, your life experiences have produced moments of anticipation, disappointment, enthusiasm, depression, ambition, laziness, passion, hope, love, hate, etc. It may seem that experiencing the whole spectrum of emotions doesn't count for much, but I would disagree. It has led to your interest in spiritual matters. These experiences have produced suffering. And suffering, ironically, is the doorway to meaning.

When suffering prods us to look more deeply into our predicament, we learn the value of loving kindness, the value of recognizing the implications of death and the value of mindfulness-awareness as an ally. What you are searching for in your travels you already found. And it was with you all the time.

Q. I raised my kids as a single mother working full time. Now they are all teenagers and I am consumed with more worry then ever about them. Perhaps my concern and love for them is over the top. I can see that this overwhelming smothering love for them isn't healthy for any of us. I know that I should give them more space, more freedom but I don't want them to fall into the same traps I fell into when I was young.

A. Knowing how to love is a very important aspect in the art of life. I am sure you know that your children will have to confront the same challenges and, regardless of what you do or say, they may make similar mistakes. That's their karma and that's how we learn. Teach them what you learned from your own experience. Guide them toward good books that will expand their understanding of the world. Good books are filled with stories concerning the pitfalls that catch us when we are not careful, honest, or ethical. Bring good people into your home. They are not emotionally involved with your kids and will be seen and listened to in a different way. It's good you now have a better perspective on things and would like to serve your family in a better way. That's praiseworthy. And, in the end, when they leave you, you will recognize that they were only *really* your kids for a short time. Then, you won't feel any sorrow when they go out the door and move on with their lives.

Q. Recently I had to look after my grandparents for five months before they passed away. They were both in their 80's. Their bodies had just worn out. I couldn't help but see how the body becomes depleted and stops running just like an old car. In the end, our body is just a burden. It's only value might be for a few spare parts, and that isn't even likely. That came as a bit of a surprise for me. I never really observed and contemplated the deterioration process from close up. It helped me a lot to now know that if I live long enough the same will happen to me. Is there something I could do to deepen my understanding of this aspect of reality?

A. Although the final episode in the dying process is obvious and utterly lucid, many people witness it without grasping the gist of the teaching. You didn't; that's praiseworthy.

The Buddha recommended that his disciples practice meditation by focusing upon the not-so-pretty aspects of the body. He taught that particular practice so that his disciples could see exactly what you observed, and more. You could make use of the practice called "*Asuba*" (Pali). It trains us to see things in a Dhamma way rather than the worldly way which struggles to cover up the ugly in order to distract us from the reality you have been observing. It is just as relevant and profound today as it was 2500 years ago. Through this practice you will deepen the insights you mentioned. Furthermore, you will come to peace and no longer fear death. Those who no longer fear death are able to live their life courageously and fully.

Q. If I understand what you have been talking about, the suffering that the Buddha talked about is not so much a natural, inherent condition but due, primarily, to the way we relate to the world. I can't quite get that. Can you talk about that?

A. I won't go too deeply into this so you don't get overwhelmed and thrown into further confusion.

Understand that the suffering is in the *looking* for happiness. We look in all the familiar places, refrigerators, the Internet, our address book, the car show, the new holiday brochures, etc. These are the familiar experiences that have lit up our interest before. We know about them and have a memory file to reexamine them in retrospect. Actually, those memory images are not very accurate, but that's another story. For now, just understand that going into the past to try and resurrect similar feelings won't work. The past is dead, the memories distorted and the future just conjecture.

Q. I know that compassion is a big factor in Buddhism. How can an ordinary person like myself increase compassion in my life? The reason this is interesting for me right now comes about because, having listened to the news for years, I read about tragedies and natural disasters such as boats sinking, railroad crashes, flooding and I feel nothing.

A.   Don't make a problem out of that. You haven't lost your sensitivity or your compassion. Your mind has taken a hiatus in the face of all the heavy stuff you have been reading about. If something were to happen to people close to you, compassion would naturally arise. Everyone tends to shut down when something very big happens. Those kinds of events are just too big to try and get a handle on. However, when something causing great pain and suffering happens in our family or the family of friends, compassion wakes up immediately.

If you want to pursue this further, meditate upon yourself, your own plight, your own weaknesses, your own regrets, and your own lack of strength to make your dreams happen. You will see the box each of us builds for ourselves. From there humility will arise and you will have an intimate feeling for compassion and a sense of how powerless we are when events overtake us. Our helplessness to prevent suffering from happening puts our life in a clearer perspective. Humility allows compassion to arise. So you can see that by bringing attention to yourself, your personal predicament becomes a catalyst for compassion.

Q.   Is depression something natural and, if so, is it something we can keep from overpowering us?

A.   I can see that lots and lots of people suffer from depression because they are so over- stimulated by games, entertainment, breaking news alerts, etc. that their mind soon droops from fatigue. Forcing the mind to be continually busy will invariably lead us to the edge of depression.

Your intuition is correct; depression doesn't really go away. It is always there ready to replace optimism, enthusiasm, attention, and eagerness. You can taste the first phase of depression whenever you don't have the energy to go on with your duties. When those rainy Mondays come around, you can feel the friction that comes with hesitancy, laziness, disinterest, and inertia wrapped up in the equation of the moment. That is low-grade depression, like when dark moods eclipse the bright sunny day. Depression is the natural result of lack of connection to Spirit, to their own Nature.

These days, people are often depressed without recognizing either the condition or the cause. Modern lifestyles have dulled them to the point where they can hardly recognize the various states of their mind. Low-grade depression becomes so familiar that they can barely recognize its presence. Often the primary cause is too much information, which has exhausted their brain. And they have been exploited by a deluge of media advertising, which has dulled the discriminating mind. The most alarming side to the overdose of information, including a deluge of soft and hard pornography, is suicide. If you haven't noticed, suicide is endemic throughout the satellite-wired world.

What we can do to maintain positive stability is to strengthen the mind. And that takes us right back to the necessity of meditation.

Q. **There are so many conflicts in this world. Why can't competent and sensitive people come to the fore to save the world from destroying itself?**

A. Many of the problems in the world are emotional issues. We tend to react emotionally with them. They are similar to husband and wife misunderstandings. Also, many of the issues creating conflicts have been interwoven in the history of different countries. They won't be solved easily. No doubt, what you have observed is that few leaders have the ability to think compassionately and comprehensively. To be a "peacemaker" leader, a person would have to encompass morality, determination, empathy, compassion and power to have any impact upon the problems of selfishness and ignorance that are pushing the world towards destruction. The development of those factors requires an extensive period of mental cultivation. Not until someone has come to this level of development can they see the nature of the world. In contemporary history we have the examples of Gandhi, Nelson Mandela, and Martin Luther King. Why don't *you* start meditating and become someone who can make a difference!

Q. **I have tried for months to get up early. I just cannot do it. So, is there a way forward for me? Why is it so hard to do?**

A. I'm not saying or suggesting that getting up early is an easy thing to do. In the beginning, to get up hours before you normally do in order to do something as subtle and refined as sitting quietly is daunting indeed. Spiritual growth is hard work, but we have to do it. If we understand what's at stake the energy will come up. Once you begin you will find that you feel well-rested on less sleep and that you have more energy to work with throughout the day. I am sure you will be able to meet the challenge when you recognize that our life needs discipline. Without discipline we are destined to suffer from confusion, dissipation, and the domination of negative emotions, which bulldozes us into danger. See the *opportunity* to meditate as primary duty. Meditating will strengthen your mind and is the supreme method for coming to see things clearly as well as avoiding mistakes. Sleeping through those fertile early morning hours is a guarantee that our life will slide towards spiritual death.

Q. **Perhaps I know too much. I am not a radical person but I am totally disgusted with my government. I do everything I can to avoid paying taxes for this war and the next one. I know most of our tax money goes to the military, so-called defense contractors, subsidies to repressive governments, domestic spy agencies, and whatnot. I have heard the axiom that one should "Caesar his due" but I cannot, in good conscience, pay the taxes imposed on my earnings. My question is, "Am I being unethical? Am I breaking the precepts by my refusal to support violations of human rights?"**

A. It depends upon what kind of standards you want to have propping up your life. Everyone lives in their own world, their own social environment. In that world we live under our beliefs. We do the best we can from where we see things. Most people have to make compromises with their integrity. Actually, they don't have to, they chose to.

As you undoubtedly recognize, there is a social and spiritual dimension to our lives. The spiritual demands harmlessness and impeccability. Our social demands are concerned with survival, not only the survival of the body but also of our beliefs.

We can easily become slaves of our political ideas and of assorted so-called education indoctrination. From where you see things, paying your taxes is immoral. From a social perspective one can say that. However, from a spiritual perspective we know that you are keeping money that doesn't belong to you. That is stealing which goes against the second precept.

In the end, you have to decide how much of your life you will allow to be dictated by your social-political standpoint and how much by your spiritual principles.

Q. **Is the body and mind one and the same thing?**

A. It seems that way. They are certainly involved with each other. But they are two distinct things.

I will tell you how I discovered the answer to your question up close and indisputably. Several years ago, while meditating in this cave, I had an encounter with a cobra that taught me this lesson. One night, while I was sitting in Samadhi, I heard a strange sound that seemed to be moving towards me. At that time, I was meditating in the smaller cave below this one which was so narrow that I had to crawl into it through a tunnel. At the end of the shaft there was an area of about one-meter by one-meter where I would sit in utter silence. This cave is deep in the mountain so no sounds from outside could enter. Without light or sound, time became almost irrelevant and I could sit for 5-6 hours at a time. Earlier in that particular night, about 6-7 large field rats ran past me, glancing my feet as they returned to their homes deep inside the mountain. I expect the snake was interested in stalking them because the cobra I met that night slithered along the same track as the rats. And because of that, I casually thought the sound I was hearing was that of a rat trotting down the tunnel. However, my mind couldn't quite fit the sound I was hearing with that of a rat running. In fact, the image that sprang into my head was that of a rat sliding toward me! That image just didn't make sense. The image that followed was that of a big snake. I immediately reached for my flashlight but knocked it over and found myself fumbling around in the dark trying to find it. When I did manage to find it, my hand had become so shaky that I had trouble flipping the switch. When I could manage the switch, I turned the light towards the tunnel. I was startled to see that the snake had come to within a foot or foot and a half of me. With the light in his face the cobra sat up, hissing and looking both frightened and menacing, staring at me as he prepared to strike at my eyes. Then he straightened up, seemingly scrutinizing me to see how much of a danger I posed and how much of an obstacle I was in his search for dinner. I could feel that he was considering options before making his decision. I closed my eyes, prepared myself to die and sent loving-kindness to the snake. I wanted him to know I meant no harm and that it was safe to be near me. I turned my heart towards the snake and sent him loving-kindness.

The most interesting part of this situation was the fact that my body was shaking like mad because it definitely didn't want to die, while my mind was rock solid and fearless. I could clearly see that the body and mind was *not* one thing. That was a fascinating in-your-face insight. The body is the body, the mind is the mind. They are interrelated and independent.

By the way, the snake backed off and I managed to escape death one more time!

So, if you want to verify what I discovered as Truth, I suggest you find a dark secluded cave and wait for your snake to arrive!

Q. **What do you say when people come to you with intense personal problems that have carried them away and can easily carry the listener away?**

A. Regardless of what I am hearing, I recognize that my responsibility to that person is to "say the right thing". Certainly some people come here who have personal melodramas that befuddle them. They often feel mired in suffering. But, since I don't see that as "persons" with "personal melodramas," I don't get emotionally involved. I just listen and allow whatever wisdom I have to say the right thing.

Q. **I always thought that when my children grew up, and established their own lives, my anxiety about them would disappear and I could feel content and relieved. It hasn't turned out like that. Even though they are all grown up and on their own I still worry about them when I haven't heard from them.**

A. I understand how your feelings are turned around from your expectations. Your confusion is common and a difficult one to rectify. *The reality is that whatever we love will bring us sorrow.* For decades, you have thought that your worries about your children were an indication that by looking after them in that way you were being a good mom. You became a kind of compulsive worrier about your kids. It all seemed right. In fact, the manner of your relationship to your kids would mean that this neurotic tendency to worry would become fixed in your mind.

Regardless of where your children are, the worry factor continues to cause distress.

Certainly, I am not suggesting that mothers abandon their relationships with their children. Rather, I suggest that they establish them in the right, skillful way. We humans have a variety of ways to love someone.

When we love with anxiety or fear, that love is certain to bring sorrow. When we love wanting something in return, someday that love will turn around and bite us. When our love is linked to demands, again, we are going to suffer the bite of dissatisfaction. There is, as we all know, romantic love. And that kind of selfish and fantasy love is certain to end in sorrow as well. At the very least, we can count on the grief that comes from separation. These are varieties of love with a small "l". They are all subject to the Truth that love makes us susceptible to heartache.

Then, there is the love with the big "L". This is Love that comes forth out of empathy and compassion. It is critical for us to know the difference and the factors that differentiate between the two. In the case of conventional love as most people know it, there is a tremendous amount of desire, wanting and ego involved. In the case of pure Love, there is no one wanting anything. There is simply the response to the-way-things-are. This is selfless Love. When the self is not controlling the situation, there is nothing for desire, wanting, fear, or pride to stick to. The response to the situation is pure. When the response is pure there is not going to be the inevitable and inescapable pain that sticks to and follows conventional love.

If you invested in conventional love, making the transition and change will take considerable time and effort. Only through seeing the truth I am presenting and training your mind to honor it will you gain release from the anxiety and tension your love causes you.

Q. **I have come to understand that I limit my life through the window I open onto life. So how do I open more windows?**

A. I don't exactly understand what you mean by windows. I know that it is an operating system for computers.

Think of it this way. I am not a mathematician, so I won't attempt to create an exact equation, but the quality, depth and expanse of your life is dependent on the power of your hidden fears, the passion charging your desires, and the intensity of your attachment to what you mistakenly believe is yours. Contrast this with the necessity for us to make intelligent and appropriate sacrifices throughout our lifetime.

Don't think so much about expanding your life as taking good care of your duties. Life will open and expand on its own. The windows and doors will open into a dimension you have yet to experience.
There are other factors and other virtues that you can develop to support your spiritual life. You will meet them along the way. First see to it that you are established in doing your duty.

On the other side of the mathematical equation there will be a number, a symbol characterizing Freedom. That freedom expresses the elegance, dignity, and magnitude of your fully-lived life.

Q. I want to help the world but the momentum of the insanity seems unstoppable. I don't want to stand up against evil forces as a "candle in the wind". What can one do in this world to stop war, starvation, abuse, exploitation, etc.?

A. A good place to begin is to see that the problems are too big for you to do much to stem the insanity. That will free you from thinking you are supposed to do something in order not to be part of the problem. Actually, many of the people doing something are, unwittingly, part of the problem. The dark forces that rule the world cannot be subdued easily or without a considerable amount of skillful energy. The mafias of leadership and wealth have more power than you think. They have no compunction against lying, cheating, and killing to keep their hold on power. Nonetheless we can and should challenge destructive energies. There are ways to do this. If you intend to be a social activist, I would suggest that you study the approach used by the Dalai Lama in his relationship with China.

Essentially, he places harmlessness and compassion before any strategy intended to serve his goals. He lives simply and in harmony with everything. This way of life is slow but it has real impact. His power is subtle, virtuous, and honorable. The lesson here is that by incorporating spiritual ideas into our work, into our life, we take the high road through this adventure.

Q.   When I was a young child one of my relatives began to sexually abuse me. I thought it was an expression of love towards me. This went on for almost four years before my parents found out about it. When they did, I was the one they blamed. They forbid me to talk about what had happened to anyone. Somehow, my memory buried these years. It was only when I left home to attend university that all this started to come back. I began to see a psychiatrist. I was in therapy for 7 years before I felt that the effects of this abuse no longer dominated my life.

Do you think that people who exploit others in this kind of way should be severely punished? Should this monster be allowed to live out his last days without any punishment, without feeling guilty for what he did?

A.   I wouldn't be too quick to condemn. What happened to you was certainly traumatic and terrible. Unless the abuser was totally insane, I am sure he has suffered considerably for this despicable behavior. People who do these kinds of things to children are seen by us as hell beings. They have the body of a human but the mind of something that came out of the hell realm.

But, for right now, let's look at this in a different way. Instead of considering the befitting punishment for something that happened a long time ago, let's just ask "why?" We know that there is karma between beings. Many Enlightened Beings believe that we have all been one another's husband-wife, mother-father, sister-brother, etc. No one can say what kind of previous relationships you had with that person. We don't know if, in previous lives, you were married, you were enemies, you killed his mother, raped his sister, tortured him in a dungeon for 40 years, or committed some similar dastardly deed.

Things in this lifetime arise as a consequence of past karma. If someone doesn't understand how karma affects their life, then punishment, guilt, forgiveness, and shame can have no real meaning. If you were able to make this person suffer, to feel guilt or shame for his actions would that change the past? Would that be of any value for you or him? Ironically guilt and shame can paralyze people. If someone is moored in a state where they are unable to either heal or develop any understanding concerning the karmic tendencies that prod and dominate them, nothing is gained. The poison that comes from holding-on continues to infect our lives. Make sure your objective is not to punish the perpetrator but to free yourself.

This doesn't minimize the wrong. Sexual abuse is certainly an awful crime which traumatizes the one who is exploited. It, necessarily, also generates heavy shame and guilt in the perpetrator. Beings who do these kinds of things are acting under the cohesion of unseen and unknown karma. It's unfortunate that judicial courts don't recognize the influence of karma. Gross felonies happen because beings are unable to control the energies manifesting out of their karmic inheritance. That should be a factor understood and factored in along with the desire to hand out punishment. If karmic element were part of the Western legal system it would be more able to adjudicate wisdom-based justice.

As for your concern, don't worry about him getting away with anything. He didn't get away with anything. Nobody gets away with anything.

Q. These days a one-time, whole-lifetime marriage is becoming more and more of a rarity. People don't necessarily think in terms of monogamy. Like the movie and rock stars, they can accept serial marriages and see each marriage as a learning experience. Do you see this as a good thing?

A. In marriage what I see as a "good thing" is love, commitment, responsibility, wisdom-based child rearing, sacrifice, and service, the creation of an environment in which the parents and children can be nurtured, taught morality, and to grow wiser. Love, spiritual love is the foundation of it all. That doesn't mean that I regard divorce and re-marriage as bad. Pragmatically, few people enter into marriage anywhere close to a willingness to serve, to sacrifice for the benefit of the other person. Few people enter marriage with the skills to make it work. As long as there isn't any conduit to transmit the lessons we need in order to live our life in an intelligent and compassionate manner, the intimate relationships between people will certainly crumble. These days the elders no longer carry these lessons to young people because they themselves never learned them. Of course, the schools don't teach people how to build successful relationships of any kind, let alone a marriage. People grow up to be young adults without any guidance as to how to relate even to themselves---their thoughts, emotions, feelings, memories and karma. The lack of this kind of education pretty much assures that most people will have great difficulty maintaining their primary relationships. So, for some, marriage and failed marriage is the route they have to take towards maturity. It's called learning the very hard way.

Q. **I don't know what's happening to me. For the past two years I have been becoming increasingly bored with everything: new clothes, new wheels, romance, vacations, money, work, sports, entertainment...you name it, it no longer does anything for me.**

A. The distractions you mentioned are no longer distracting! If you really look at the things that used to distract you, you find that you were always compelled to move on from one distraction to another in order to maintain interest in things. Without these distractions, you can see the fact that the world *is* boring. If everything didn't lead to boredom it wouldn't be the world. That which is beyond the world, the present moment, where no one is as one thinks they are, is the un-boring. The present is fascinating in a subtle and refined way.

Because the world is intrinsically repetitive and boring, people are continuously searching. They find something of interest, then lose interest in it, then search again. And again. And again. You have matriculated out of the realm of diversion-entertainment. Now what?

Now you're ready to meditate, to serve, to sacrifice, and to offer yourself to the Truth.

Q.   **I have just come to understand just how many things anyone can get addicted to: alcohol, drugs, praise, pain, work, sleep, music, sex, golf, cigarettes, gambling, etc. In a book I just read, the author mentioned all kinds of addictions. The author defined addiction as some activity someone is compulsively drawn to repeat. His hypothesis was that the cultural influences determine whether or not someone is likely to become an addict. Does that premise make sense to you?**

A.   Every kind of addiction, as I see it, has two components. One, a kind of inherent addiction from previous lives. If someone has previously been addicted to something or other, they are likely to come into this birth with that tendency. This factor is dependent upon karma. It's a strange fact that most people live their lives exchanging one kind of bondage, one addiction for another.

The second factor concerns strength of mind. This factor is dependent totally on mind development through proper meditation. It is the factor that fortifies the mind thereby protecting us from mischievous influences. The mind that has not developed strength is a weak and vulnerable mind. A weak mind is powerless and a powerless mind is a dangerous thing. A weak mind has very little ability to access or utilize wisdom; it is fertile ground for compulsive and unskillful thoughts. Now, when a thought arises in a powerless mind which suggests that we can find some happiness by doing some kind of destructive behavior such drinking, gambling, or overeating, that mind is prone to completely believe the thought and impulsively pursue the idea. The more often we couple this thought with action, the deeper it goes, and the more malicious it becomes. If the mind were made strong, it could brush off these dangerous thought forms. When our mind is strong we can control and subdue all insensitive and uncaring trains of thought. With a strong mind we can see the long-term consequences of our choices in comparison to the short term relief offered by things in the world. We are not going to be tricked into believing addictive activities hold no risk. Here wisdom intervenes for our benefit. So you see that the strength of the mind is the decisive factor. It protects us by launching wisdom.

The author of the book you read probably talks about how addiction to, say, drugs generates a physiological addiction response as well as a psychological one. I just brought your attention to the psychological aspect because it is the mind that is dominant. Everything that happens in the body has originated first in the mind and then flowed down into the body.

You might ask, "Why does somebody choose to devote the time and energy to meditation practice?" The answer is "boon". "Boon" is the Goodness factor that comes out of an accumulation of skillful and selfless actions performed in the past. It is this "boon" which initiates and is the catalyst for developing wisdom-compassion. If you don't want to be addicted to drugs, ideology, philosophy, views and opinions, meditate your mind.

This is all you need to know about addictions. However, this is a subject that has wide implications...contemplate upon it.

Q. **Why is it that the schools in the West don't teach students about the effect of karma on our lives? Why aren't kids informed about the effect of their actions? If kids understood that they carry karma from the past into this life, they would be less inclined to want to do unskillful and harmful things to themselves and others.**

In some places they are still debating whether the world was created in 7 days. Recognizing the influence of karma is light years away from that hypothesis.

You bring up a critical point. It's very unfortunate that this aspect of our life is neglected because every one of us is a karmic condition. Regardless of whether we understand anything about this state of affairs, karma will exert a tremendous effect upon our lives. Karma doesn't care if you believe in it or not. That's why it is critical for us to understand the machinery and workings of karma and then to work to transcend it. In short, karma is something we need to understand in order to sever ourselves from it. Obviously, kids need training in their youth in mind development. However, even though modern day students learn all the rules concerning spelling, mathematics, and football, they don't know much about themselves. Kids are further and further away from Nature and orthodox education doesn't acknowledge karma as a powerful factor in our life and probably never will. But the effect of failing to notice this aspect of life is like training a car mechanic without providing any instructions on how the engine works! "The Primary Laws of Life" is universally unavailable. Governments are, at the least, negligent in regard to this critical curriculum. This omission is a big part of the conspiracy to keep us from knowing what is what and how the world works. Ultimately, this concerns the nature of freedom. In understanding what true freedom is, the mundane concerns that drive economies and initiate wars would get set aside. The *gross national happiness* that would replace the conventional reality would encourage fidelity, responsibility, bonding, and service. The development of wisdom and compassion would become the priorities.

Karma demands a critical "under-standing" for, in fact, we stand under it.

Q.   **After three years, I am still grieving the loss of a lover. This depression is like a sandbag that weighs on me and obstructs my very breath. This weight never seems to go away, even in sleep.**

A.   It needn't go away. You need only to go away from it. Decide that enough is enough. Let the universe, let your mind understand this in no uncertain terms. There is something in you that still wants to hold on to the past. Perhaps this thing you still value is in memories, or your identity in that relationship. Whatever has you buying into it, release yourself from it. LET GO!

This won't be the end of the story until you make use of meditation in order to sharpen your mind so that you don't get caught into this kind of reverie mixed with illusion ever again. Through the process of healing you will learn that Happiness is a non-dependent sort of thing that arises from within.

Q. **What do you mean by letting go? What am I supposed to let go of? Myself? How can anyone do that?**

A. We let go of things that don't belong to us which we mistakenly think do belong to us. We attach to things that go through the mind, images, our notions of personality, our age, our nationality, etc. taking them as personal. And there are virulent side effects. For instance when we attach to memory in the ordinary way, we buy into conventional time and space. Whenever you are engaged, fascinated, enchanted with something, you will forge an attachment. Here too, you are caught in the trap of time and space. You go beyond time and space as soon as you let go. When you go beyond time and space you are free. Freedom is from something.

Q. **Since graduating six years ago I have had a string of disappointing jobs. They offered me no challenge, were clearly dead end jobs, or were full of boring people I felt alienated from. What can I do to change my fortune?**

A. I am not a fortune teller. I can only remind you that you are a karmic condition, just like all of us. Some aspects of your life will go easily and some with difficulty. You could live a long time in good health, develop nurturing relationships, associate with spiritual friends, and enjoy wonderful parents. Or, it could all be just the opposite. Easy or hard. What is better? Actually, difficulty and conflict will teach you a lot more than pleasure and ease.

Anyway, don't make a problem out of this aspect of your life. As I listened to your story this afternoon, I could tell that you are physically and mentally strong, and well educated. You have the opportunity to travel and observe life in other cultures, and you even found your way into this cave temple. Earlier, you mentioned that you have a fine family that supports you in whatever you do. All in all, you are unlucky in small ways but lucky in big ways. Don't try and wish away difficulty, work with it. Finally, contemplate that many of the people who have accomplished the most to improve the current of social thought and behavior toward the Good have struggled through decades of setbacks, failure and defeats, frustration, disappointment, and fear.

Q. **Is it possible to live a life that doesn't roller coaster between highs and lows?**

A. There is a Path to a life that flows in blissful equanimity, and that kind of life is a life you can fashion for yourself.

Q. **My life seems to be just a merry-go-round of problems, problem solving, anticipation and disappointment, some highs followed by a disproportionate amount of lows. The months have now turned into years. I have been caught in this cycle too long. How do I break out!**

A. If you mean break out through some magic that allows you to live exactly as you do now but without the negative, boring and unpleasant bits, you need to find a genie. What you are talking about is the dullness that defines most people's lives. Most people would say, "that's life". The fact is that you cannot control external factors in some extraordinary manner that will side-step all the difficulties and pain that we humans must deal with, notably, birth, aging, illness and death. If you wish to have as smooth and trouble-free a life as possible, you need to commit to the principles that allow that to happen: morality, discipline, sobriety, groundedness, compassion, intuitive wisdom. With these factors as allies, you are continually inclining towards the simple, the sacred and wisdom-compassion. You won't avoid the four great teachers I mentioned but you certainly will avert a great deal of irritation. If you adhere to the principles supporting harmlessness, your time in this lifetime will not be wasted.

Q.   **The world is going to Hell in a basket. People are killing each other, blowing their neighbors to pieces, devising weapons of mass destruction. I don't see any point in doing anything in this ridiculous world.**

A.   What has that got to do with you? What if everything here was ideal? What if everywhere you turned there were strawberries, Hagen Das, champagne, and gourmet chocolate bars. If everyone lived in penthouses and owned Ferrari's and personal Lear jets, wouldn't there still be the problem of jealousy, lust, envy, disappointment, aging and death, unhappiness, enduring one's karmic situation, misunderstanding concerning the nature of life, and the problem of controlling our emotions?

Some of us look at the current affairs in the world as a reminder of just how dangerous this world is and just how dangerous people can be to one another. This is a world where people kill each other over a book of matches, a broken pencil. Something as small as a mosquito has killed countless beings, and transmittable diseases of all kinds are rampant. That's good for the evening news team. What makes headline news is death. Death is the event which has the biggest impact on the human psyche but few people understand its significance from a spiritual perspective.

As meditators, we strive to understand the implication and full impact of death. Death is a reality. There is no "spin" to death. Intuitively and through our meditation practice we can understand that death and life are intimately connected. When something ends, that ending marks the beginning of the next thing. Is this a reality? Many wise people believe so. If there is new life after death, what does that imply? What does that say about the old life? It says that there is a continuum. This life connects to the next one. What crosses over? Perhaps some murky memories, perhaps some character traits. According to the law of karma, the primary aspect that carries into the new birth is the old karma, and with the old karma comes the duty, the responsibility of going beyond that karmic force in order to stop the authority of karma from driving us into life and life after life after life.

The only factor that can clear karma is wisdom. Only meditation provides the opportunity to cultivate wisdom effectively and systemically. To thirst for wisdom requires some wisdom. Fortunately, the wisdom from our past lives is embedded in the new life. Therefore, the development of wisdom is the energy we must cultivate. External conditions are perceptions in consciousness. Regardless of where you are, regardless of what's happening in the cable news world, we are obliged to cultivate wisdom and grow ourselves out of this mess. So whether the world will end in five minutes or go on indefinitely or whether life becomes so confused, so absurd to the point that the planet implodes, nothing changes. For we each personally have the same work before us. Don't let the misery of this world crush your spirit. Cultivate your inner light and let others bathe in it.

Q. **I know that life is hard. And I find meditation is hard to the extreme. Why should anyone just make the struggle to survive even more difficult?**

A. Hard? Yes. But isn't there a law that states that we have to go through the near impossibility to win the important rewards? There are moments in our lives that are really, really difficult. When we endure these moments, when we grow through them, our humanity evolves and we mature as a person. Don't be put off by the difficult. Meditation is not an art that is beyond your capability. And by becoming adept, your rectified perspective on life will assure that you free yourself from the straitjacket which has constricted your life and reduced your options. Many people work, drink cheap alcohol, eat, and sleep. Do you really think we should endeavor just to survive or is life about living?

Q. **I recently returned from my first meditation course. The teacher was encouraging us to find and recognize Bodhicitta, which I later learned is the primordial mind ground. However, throughout the retreat I kept thinking about Bobby Citta. My mind is really perverse and unsympathetic to my spiritual aspirations. How can I cure this problem?**

A. Is this the name of some rock star? You convert data into ideas that amuse you. This is the inner comedian at work. Anyway, this habit prevents you from seeing things that are new. In any case, indeed, you are far off the mark. And with those images dancing in your mind, you don't have a prayer of seeing the mind ground. That's the bad news. The good news is that this is curable. Everything is curable. Don't fret. The mind is just trying to embarrass you, trying to dissuade you from pursuing meditation. Don't get into thinking and believing you are hopeless. If you do, the pernicious energies will have duped you into surrender.

Q.   **You have been a monk for more than 20 years and yet you admit to not yet being an Enlightened being. Why is that?**

A.   I incline my life towards doing good and living with nobility. Like you, what I have going for me is the Goodness I cultivated in the past. In Thailand, we call that "boon". When we begin a journey, none of us can be certain of just how far we can go---especially when our journey is along the unknown spiritual Path. We are obliged to do the best we can for ourselves and others. The safest track to follow, in order to live within that responsibility, is to follow the footsteps of the Masters. I am still following their footsteps.

Q.   **Why is it that neighboring countries fight so many wars against each other? Is there a Buddhist way to solve the conflict between Israel and Palestine, Ireland and England, 6-8 African countries?**

A.   That has been a recurrent question. We have no magic wand to dissolve wars, but we can explain them. The kind of entrenched conflicts you are concerned about won't be solved. Perhaps they will be outgrown. It seems to me that the real issue in all wars is not about land boundaries that the news channels talk about but the control of people's minds. If you characterize someone else as "other", you will believe that they think differently, and by implication, pose a threat to you and your family. Then, it's time to consider a pre-emptive strike. The instigating factor is fear, rather than desire. When people have no fear, nothing to defend, the armies will disband and everyone can turn their attention to the problem of birth and death. When they solve that, they can sit in the park and watch the seasons change.

Supposing all the leaders everywhere practiced meditation to the point where they understood that we are not who we think we are. The practice teaches us not to believe our thoughts. Ideas are thoughts. So, all the conventional ideas of who we think we are lose much of their power. If we are not who we think we are, then you are not who I think you are. Problem solved.

Q.   I fell in love with a man who thrives on all kinds of things that totally turn me off. If not for the fact that I love him to death I couldn't see myself involved with him at all. What is this about?

A.   Would you kindly elaborate?

Q.   He loves cheap, greasy food, bars, boxing, wrestling, cigarettes, cheap beer, and vulgar pinup girls. All of this turns me off. I should mention that I have been a vegetarian for 6 years and have been practicing yoga and karate for 3 years. I have lived the "Sex in the city" lifestyle so I am hardly innocent or, what's the word, fazed.

A.   Your friend is entangled in a cluster of crude habits and infantile distractions. If you look carefully at the things that interest him, you can see that they are all things that resonate at the lowest chakra. I expect he is a big fan of porn movies and Internet gambling. I can understand why you would be disconcerted by his behavior and your own affiliation with him. When you ask yourself "how did I get into a relationship with someone like this?", you can expect that the answer can only be "karma". Karma got you in, karma will take you out. Eventually, the energy that bonds you together will exhaust itself. But don't run out and celebrate too quickly. You don't know what's waiting for you in the queue. As long as you are alive conditions will continually change. People will come and go. Some of the people you will interact with will have loveable characteristics. Some will have strange or puzzling traits. All the people you relate to are people you have karma with. They too are working things out with you. Some will find strange things about you that will set them wondering how they came to interact in your world.

Q. **I have been aggressively, and I stress AGGRESIVELY, chasing all the sensual avenues of happiness. I used to feel saturated with happiness. Then, suddenly, no matter what I do I end up feeling unsatisfied, frustrated, confused and empty. What is going on...I don't get it.**

A. The kind of hopeless happiness you have been chasing will eventually lead you over a cliff. You keep desperately poking at the world trying to maintain some kind of doomed-to- failure happiness. If you do that for long enough that small "h" happiness that you are addicted to will flip over and bite you. The kind of unhappiness you describe is the result of your craving and your greed. Stop craving. Live simply. Find ways to help others. The real Happiness will come into your life and displace all your frenetic chasing around.

Q.   How do you know how to answer questions?

A.   I try and keep out of the way. I don't answer them. Situations are relative and unique. Response must be determined by wisdom, not thought. Just say the "right thing". Actually, I am not telling anybody something they don't already know. Wisdom is real. The same Wisdom "belongs" to all of us.

Q.   What is the best way to relate to others?

A.   If there were a formula, I would say H plus C equals A. Humility plus Compassion equals Appropriateness.

Q. Supposing someone would be able to get everything they wanted continuously without interruption for their whole life, wouldn't that bliss and euphoria be wonderful? I mean like that's what we're all trying to do, isn't it? We listen to our music, drink with our friends, and meet new lovers. That's my idea of ultimate happiness.

A. I don't think you thought this through. The Buddha said that understanding where problems live in the mind and cutting that part out will bring ultimate Happiness. One has to decide if one regards this statement as worth investigating. We have faith that the Buddha told it as it is. What do you think? Was the Buddha a genius at understanding the way the mind works or was the Buddha mouthing hip-hop?!

Q. I have been in and out of five relationships over the past eight years. Three or four months after they begin they start to crumble. I have never been able to figure out why. It's not that I'm not serious, I am. I try and make my partner happy and I expect them to make me happy as well. They don't.

A. Obviously you are working with a deeply flawed hypothesis. Your idea on what makes a relationship sustain and grow is way off. I sense that you are actually taking about "gratification" when you say "happy". If you think the other person is there for your pleasure, very soon you will be left with just a sad, broken-hearted country song to remind you of the relationship.

Relationships work when both parties do their duty, and take care of their responsibilities. It certainly will help if one or both parties understand that their relationship is not about satisfaction because things certainly won't be satisfactory much of the time. You're expecting someone to bring you sensual gratification. You are deluded in thinking others can solve all your problems, make you comfortable, and gratify all your wants the instant they arise. Other people won't do that because they can't. Looking for your idea of happiness is like chasing after your shadow. The great masters have all pointed to letting go as the way to go. Let go of expectation, hope, disappointment, magic, romantic love, dreams of great wealth, winning the Noble Peace Prize, etc. Learn to let go and the next relationship will be the one you have been looking for---the one with your own Nature!

Q. **At the moment of Enlightenment does some kind of chemical reaction happen in the brain which turns someone into a spiritual genius?**

A. I don't know anything about the kind of chemistry you are talking about. Enlightenment is a radical, irrevocable change. It arises through the meditation synergy that forces all karma to disappear and all defilements to be vanquished. We cannot even say "someone" changes for the "someone" who was there before has been conquered. What is there after Enlightenment is not a someone who is a genius, but no-one who attaches to nothing.

Q. **I was obliged to attend two funerals of two business men who I knew were dishonest and exploitive people. Still, when the bodies were being lowered into the ground I began sobbing. This is not the first time this happened. It just seems very strange for me to be crying at funerals even when I don't know the guy or even if I knew the dude to be not such a nice guy.**

A.   It is natural for the body to cry out of sympathy, out of fear, or out of empathy. Our bodies don't ever want to die. However, it is critical to your happiness that you recognize that the mind and body is not the same thing. We can see feeble and worn-out people lying in ICU's everywhere connected to a half a dozen drips supporting their fragile life and yet still struggling to remain in that body. If any one of us takes the trouble to investigate their minds we would surely come to understand the way things operate in this realm. Ultimately we will not be tricked into believing that this is the end of the road and that this body is worth retaining. Remember seeing movies when the hero is giving his soliloquy before going off to his next life? He is content and at peace. He doesn't want that body any more. Sometimes the hero is all shot up and writhing in pain. As the body has its own consciousness, it is agitated and doesn't want to die but our hero knows it's time to move on and is at peace.

It's natural for us to react to the death of one of our own kind. As many times as I have watched autopsies, my legs still feel unsteady in the presence of death. This is just the way we are hard wired.

Q.   **I have been care-taking my uncle for some months now. He lives in a retirement community. I noticed that events and tours are organized for just about everyday of the week. If I had to run around to everything that's going on I would collapse in a week. Yet some couples there are busy from early morning to late night with golf, gambling tours, parties, and the like. I haven't been there long enough to see anyone collapse from all the frenetic entertainment, but I'm sure these schedules are certain to finish off a lot of these people.**

A. People work hard to postpone the inevitable. They fill their retirement with distraction, entertainment, and the pursuit of leisure. You would think that they would see the need to be still and to contemplate their life and their inescapable demise. They just carry on in the same self-oriented mode seeking the same sort of self- gratification they've always sought. They remain totally unprepared for death.

Actually, when we reach retirement our duties change. No longer do we need to think about supporting our families. Now we need to turn our mind towards spiritual matters. For people who ignore this obligation, the day will come when the energy to suppress the inevitable abates and the inevitable becomes imminent. All that they can do is struggling to live. That's just the way it is for many people.

Q. **It's been almost two years since a dear one of mine passed away. It seems like all this time I have just been trying to digest his sudden death. For a long time I was depressed. Then, suddenly, I felt angry. I don't know what's going on. This feeling of anger also makes me feel guilty. I feel guilty for being angry and guilty for having survived! What can I do to help myself?**

A. What you can do to help yourself is to understand that the stages you are going through are normal. Perhaps they are more pronounced and go on longer than they do for most people. Still, because there was deep-rooted attachment, the death of your loved one has thrown you into an abyss of pain, depression, anger, loneliness, guilt, etc. The root cause is the attachment. Extracting yourself from the attachment means that you will have to go through the stages you are experiencing. Often, the first stage is denial. We refuse to accept the facts. Then there may be depression, followed by the anger you are speaking about. Soon you will arrive at acceptance and your life will move on. This process you are going through occurs not only when someone dies, but whenever there is attachment and then the inevitable separation. In a milder form, people experience this after a divorce or when events separate them by long distances or long periods of time.

Q. **Looking back I can now see that I made many, many mistakes in my life. Intentionally and unintentionally I have hurt many people including my parents, my children, and some of my friends. I am prepared to take the consequences. Is there something I can do to help make up for my inconsideration and arrogance?**

A. The one thing that invariably arises from mistakes is regret. You are suffering from the effects of regret now. So don't think that your heedless actions have gone unpunished. The feeling of regret *is* punishment. The past is over. You can't do anything about it. If you truly want to atone for your mistakes, determine to put your life on a moral and ethical footing. Your own life will improve and your admirable evolution will inspire others to skillfully align their lives as you have done.

Your past mistakes have taken you to this moment in time. The mistakes and the learning that came out of your mistakes have brought on the maturity I see in you. Mistakes initiate the learning process. No one is born smart. We all have to start from almost nothing. If you truly wish to avoid the regret and shame that comes from mistakes, determine to act unselfishly in the present moment through mindfulness and awareness. Living in this way, arrogance will be replaced with humility and inconsideration with compassion.

Q.   Why is there always war?

A.   Because there are always armies. It is interesting to note that governments go to war for peace! Once they have established a powerful army, they rationalize the need to conquer or subdue some area of strategic interest in order to preserve or expand their idea of peace.

The results inevitably lead to conquered people wanting more autonomy, more religious freedom, more political freedom, a bigger share of the wealth, religious law, etc. The next war arises out of the earlier conquest. Where is the source of the problem? Wanting. We can see that the problem is in wanting and the subsequent problems that arise, arise in wanting as well.

All the leaders on this planet need to understand that war is a problem in the human mind. Essentially, not a problem concerning territory, minerals, fish, oil, or trees. The mind is not at peace, it wants, it craves, it fears. In trying to settle these problems from outside, there will be aggression, there will be war. Mind-made problems are pervasive. Whether it is war with one's neighbor, one's partner, one's colleagues, or with a country on the other side of the planet, until there is peace there will be war.

When war is no longer a consideration and peace and harmony reign in the mind, then war is over for that being.

Q.   **What is luck?**

A.   From a Dharma sense, luck is karma. Or it could be the intervention of angels, which is really the same thing. It doesn't arise by chance, just as bad luck doesn't arise by chance. There are underlying conditions that generate it. We always get what we deserve as the universe puts things right. The notion of luck arises from misunderstanding. It suggests arbitrariness. Here in Thailand there is a whole industry of sidewalk and late night TV astrologers whose sole function seems to be to let their customers know how long it will take before they become rich. If we understand that the conditions for good luck come from our good behavior, we won't ever be disappointed, heart-broken, or bemused by hope.

Q.   I have recently become interested in history, world history. It has given me a deeper understanding of how events on this planet unfold. And, therefore, my expectations that things will or can get better have largely been discarded. One significant thread that runs through world history is that after a war, the losers seek to find ways to avenge themselves and to recover what they see as theirs. So, in time, they will fight again. And if the other side loses what they learned to regard as theirs, they too will re-ignite a war. And so it goes on and on. Is this the working of karma?

A. Indeed. And, *everything* is the working of karma. That is why it is said that the world will spin on endlessly as these sorts of events carry on with their own energy of anger, retribution, and righteous indignation.

If I were ruler of this world and could make laws and determine punishment, I would make all motivation, all actions based on somebody or some group trying to get even by harming people or their property in order to avenge a perceived wrong, the absolutely heaviest criminal offense. I would make it a capital offense even to incite others to avenge anything whatsoever. That all encompassing universal law alone would reduce the insanity fueling the deaths of hundreds of thousands of people a year who have gotten caught up in the hallucination that the past needs to be offset, that honor is at stake, or that there is a "final solution" that can be settled towards anything whatsoever in the world. And, in particular, that law would target any charismatic person intending to manipulate others into believing in his or her view of right and wrong. Infamous characters who come to mind include Hitler, Pol Pot, Milosevic, Pinochet, Amin, etc. These kinds of people can be considered to be the most dangerous kind of infectious organisms on the face of the earth. (I am talking this way in order to make a point. Do you get the point?)

Q. **It looks to me that Western governments are determined to set up democracies everywhere and bring free elections to everyone in the world. Is this going to solve the problem of poverty, terrorism, and spiritual development?**

A. I suspect you know the answer to your question as well as I. Without sounding too cynical, shouldn't we understand what freedom really is before importing flawed ideologies everywhere? Is democratic freedom such as we are seeing in America, the U.K, Australia, etc. *real* freedom? Will the opportunity to choose one of 2-3 mediocre candidates reduce or eliminate the problem of greed, anger, and ignorance? I doubt it. Importing democratic institutions often makes life far more difficult by building superstores, malls and stimulating consumerism. Following that comes debt and the international money lenders, western medicines which, due to their devious side effects, generate a robust health industry, Johnny Walker, weight-loss therapies, etc. etc. Incidentally, the problem of poverty stems from the mistaken belief that cheap labor is a clever strategy for making the rich richer. Actually, if the poor had money they would be buying things and the rich would get even richer. Does someone have to be a monk to figure that out?

Q. **I am a teacher and I certainly recognize the importance of what you are saying. If you had the opportunity to teach young children just one thing, what would that be?**

A. You might guess it would be meditation. However, rather than try and teach them to meditate, I believe it would be better for them to first understand the outstanding qualities that they can develop as a human being and for them to understand which attributes are respected by good people everywhere. For instance, we human beings respect generosity, compassion, commitment to one's duties, and selflessness. Also, what are the attributes of a good friend? They should learn early that we can tell what kind of person somebody is by what they say when they are angry, by how they spend their money and their time. That which has the greatest impact on children is the behavior of their parents. But, if I am to stay with one thing, I have to stop here.

Q.   **I met a very interesting person some months ago, and we started a relationship. From that time all kinds of strange and unusual circumstances keep occurring. For instance, I met someone on a ferryboat in Greece that I hadn't seen for 15 years just one day after I came upon his picture in an old album. I had missed the earlier boat because the taxi broke down. This man's (my new boyfriend) mother's maiden name is the same as a friend I had back in kindergarten (who drowned in a swimming pool while still a child), I won a door prize at a party we went to by chance, my computer crashed and 10 minutes later a new tenant in my apartment house knocked at my door to borrow a mop. It just so happened that he was a computer expert and had my machine up and running in 15 minutes. I had a dream one night that someone would pick me up in a new red SUV. The next day while I was waiting for my bus, a colleague I work with but had hardly ever talked to saw me on the corner, pulled his brand new red SUV over to the curb and picked me up. There are other events, as well. Gathering all this together I am sure this weird situation is way off the statistical charts. What is this about this person?**

A.   Who says the cause is this new person? Causes and conditions are infinite. Don't make too much of this. It is interesting. So what? Let go.

Q. I have seen the word "profound" thrown around a lot. The professors who teach the arts and literature courses I am taking like to praise certain writers and painters as "profound and philosophical intellects". When I read their books I don't think I am directly touching spirituality. When you say profound, what are you alluding to?

A. It's not all that complex. It is very simple. By profound I mean that something has given us a look into Nature itself. It is realization which is in alignment with Truth. Many of the great writers have had profound insights. However, when their insight is transmitted onto paper something distinctive is bound to be lost. You, as the reader, have to try to restructure the natural truth the writer is presenting. It gets complicated.

Q. Several months ago I was diagnosed with a life threatening disease. Since then I have turned my attention more and more towards spirituality.

A. This situation has pushed your life into introspection. This is your great opportunity to know your life, to know who you are. Start with fear. You can easily get in touch with the anxiety about facing the possibility of looming death. You're here now, in fear. Then, there is the unknown, the abysses which you must cross to get to freedom from fear. With freedom from fear comes freedom from wanting. You will see that most fear is mind-induced and is intimately connected with wanting. Some fear is in the body; it doesn't want to die. Don't be concerned with that survival-fear. As you scrutinize the fear-wanting dynamic you will be able to let go and dislodge fear. When fear and wanting are no longer blocking the healing process, you will have given your body the best chance to heal itself and you will have taken yourself to a new level of maturity. This is the best you can do for yourself. And because it is totally pro-active, you won't get caught in cherishing your illness.

Q. **Why do the forest monasteries have signs requesting "Silence"? If you are always silent how will anything ever get done?**

A. We regard silence as noble. We don't really have to talk to get what needs to be done, done. The "Silence" we enforce is not an absolute silence. It means you don't talk when there is no need for talk. You don't chat, you don't argue politics, and you don't vent your irritation at the price of beans. In the temple one can discover that just by being silent, we can learn a lot about ourselves.

Q. **I don't see the value in life. You are born, you die. What goes down in the middle of that is of little consequence.**

A. First, let me tell you that only the unreal dies. Second, let me tell you that death is the precursor to life. You can place your bets on the fact that a next life will follow this one. (See www.next-life.com) Life has meaning; it has value. There is always the opportunity to cultivate Goodness. Goodness is real stuff, it doesn't die. When you understand that your life has given you the opportunity to develop Goodness, you will certainly come to respect and esteem your human birth.

Q. I was in Indonesia at the time of the big tsunami. It was shocking to see people doing all kinds of things that were inappropriate to the crisis. Some people running around collecting all kinds of little things of no consequence that were ruined by the water. Other people standing around in groups jabbering away when help for the injured was needed. I could clearly see that most people can't handle much apart from the everyday circumstances of their lives. At the time of the tsunami most people were running around like chickens with their heads cut off, or were stunned into uselessness or hopelessness.

A. In those kinds of situations we can see who has cultivated their mind and who hasn't. Those who have, have presence-of-mind. They can appreciate the situation and do what is appropriate and is in step with their abilities. The wisdom and compassion that is cultivated through meditation practice covers all layers, all dimensions of a situation.

Q. A few hundred years ago there were only a few hundred million people on this planet. Now there are 6 billion. How can there be an increase of people? How can the number of souls increase?

A. There are no souls, as such. The energy that manifests into people with bodies arises out of karma, for these bodies and minds (in fact) are karmic conditions. Energy is infinite. The number of beings, seen and unseen is infinite. If you think in terms of Adam and Eve being the father and mother of the whole race of humans, you will become baffled by the mathematics.

Instead of starting there, start with the concept that this world is beginning-less and endless. The understanding of this view is something beyond our ability to understand.

Q. **What is meditation practice for?**

A. The evolution of mind. It is for evolving the mind. Without meditation, the mind becomes weakened and more coarse. With meditation practice, the mind becomes more refined, quicker, lighter, more flexible, and more energetic.

Q. **I presume there are advantages to living in a monastery. Obviously life is quieter and simpler. But how does one do the things people do in the world, social service, raising the future generation of people, creating and designing things to make life easier in a Wat?**

A. The everyday world is a playground for doing a million and one things. There are endless interesting things to do. There are endless important things to do in the world, but are they important enough? Most people choose to try and do the things you mentioned. We here in the monastery incline our lives toward doing nothing. Before you condemn this undertaking, I suggest you contemplate on it. The nothing I am talking about is actually "no-thing."

Q. I feel as though I have as good a life as possible. My grandmother died and left me a trust fund, I have a nice apartment where I have many friends, I am able to travel anywhere I want whenever I want, my health is fine, I don't feel like my childhood experiences are any kind of problem. I even have a really fine girlfriend that respects and loves me. You know what I am going to say next! My life still feels like it's going nowhere and does not make me feel content.

A. You may have as pleasurable and comfortable a life as possible but it is still a life. You aren't likely to feel content with your life until you know who you are and why you are here. That is what meditation is about. It also frees you from who you think you are, and the bewilderment concerning what to do here, and why we are obliged to do it.

Q. I have many options as to how to use my leisure time. But, when I follow these options I find that I am worn out and in the end, still feel like something important is missing in my life.

A. It has been said by some wise person that "we never get enough of what we don't need". Set about trying to understand what this means and it will get you past your present predicament.

Q. "Happiness" is an enigma to me. Somehow I think there is a magic state of mind that can bring it about at will. I think my mind is not powerful enough to figure it out.

A. You're overlooking the obvious. Happiness comes from suffering--getting beyond suffering. It is the feeling you get when you are above or beyond suffering. It doesn't depend on where you are or what you are doing. It doesn't depend on anything.

Q. Then, what I hear is that we have a license to live carelessly and negligently so one can reap the suffering!

A. Yes. You're free to do any stupid thing that comes into your mind. You will suffer for your stupidity and you may learn from the pain. But, then again, maybe you are too stupid to learn and just go on and on oblivious to the harm and pain factors. In that case, you get to be reborn in the deepest hell realms where the lessons are the most horrendous and intolerable. The "wheel" doesn't really care how long or how painful your journey becomes.

Q. A lot of traumatic events happened in my childhood. Most of them concerned my parents and some concerned my two brothers. As an adult, even after years of psychotherapy, I am still not really able to live a constructive and happy life. I am very angry with my family. I know that they are to blame for my situation and yet I wonder if all those years of trauma was just my destiny?

A. Don't blame anyone. All events are karma. We are here to learn from them. Your family had no more opportunity to behave differently than a moth flying around a fire. Don't assign blame. Rather, see that life is a university. We are here to learn our lessons and get beyond.

Q. How do I use meditation to see into the deepest dimensions of my life? And what will I find when I get there?

A. You could develop sufficient concentration to take apart a mind moment. Your concentration will enable you to see the present moment and you will see that there is layer after layer after layer of stuff preventing you from seeing-things-as-they-are. When you let go of wanting and fear you are able to go deeper. Ultimately you can only arrive at the deepest dimension by letting go of the biggest barrier, the idea of who-you-think-you-are. While you begin trying to discover something for yourself, you end by shedding the idea of self. Your investigation will be an odyssey to freedom. Freedom from who-you-think-you-are. What will you find when you get there? No one, doing nothing.

Q. My wife is a Bangkok Thai who has been well educated. Still, she is afraid to be alone because that's when ghosts come to eat people and she is afraid to be in dark places or in the countryside because there she would be vulnerable to the kinds of ghosts that slither up your legs and then nibble on your stomach. I knew country people had these notions but I was surprised to see it so strongly in my wife.

A. People who have seen ghosts believe in them. People who haven't, don't. The question of whether ghosts exist or not is a very interesting one. But the issue of fear is more important. Most of us have been set up to be afraid. Afraid of the dark, strangers, car-jackers, scam artists, people standing behinds us in the elevator, villains waiting in ambush for us to jog on by. Now, we are supposed to worry about terrorists. This is all very good for governments because they can initiate Big Brother security on our behalf. Certainly, secular education doesn't teach people not to be afraid. Or that fear is a generated condition which one doesn't have to believe in. The same can be said for the conventional education system which encourages students to want more and more unnecessary and unusable things. Obsessive wanting, too, is a generated condition. Apart from our need for food, medicine, shelter, emotional sustenance, and clothing, excessive wanting generates a whole cycle of problems for us.

This is a good example for both of you to see that within the standard educational system ideas are suggested and reinforced. These ideas propagate the notions and myths we live by and how we experience the world. We become acculturated through conventional education, through movies, etc. After that, the mischief-making aspect of our imagination takes over and so a being ends up as a perfectly formed frightened, inflexible, and docile adult.

Q.   **What I have been discovering through meditation practice is that things are not as they seem. For instance, I have always believed that what I see is what there is to see. As things impact my eyes, my mind then makes "sense" of these images. Now that I have watched my mind in a meditation retreat, I know that what I perceive is tainted and not reliable at all.**

A.   You're on the right track. Congratulations, you have learned a lot in a short period of time. You can see how we are trapped in habitual misunderstanding, and that our senses can no longer be trusted. For instance, our eyes appear to observe an image at the eyeballs. Then this image is transferred to our memory data bank, which compares and contrasts the image in light of previous images. We then fix an identity onto this image through the filters in this mechanical process. The *feeling* of this moment of consciousness is lost in the rush to identify the image.

The *feeling*, if you stop following thoughts, beliefs, and habits, will lead you out of your eyeballs, and you will see things without the intervention of your memories, hopes, desires, fears etc. You will see things fresh, as they are.

Q. **I live in a big city and work the compulsory 9 hours a day. When you add in the 2-3 hour commute you can understand that there are days when I hardly see the sun. When I arrive home, I am worn out. I rarely exercise and eat food that can be warmed in the microwave. I don't need anyone to tell me that there isn't much to my life. When could I possibly meditate? In the early morning when my body feels so heavy that I can hardly drag myself out of bed at the last moment in order to get to work on time? Or at night when I come home from the commute exhausted?**

A. O.K. You are living some kind of virtual life and need to go back to basics. I suggest you begin by trying to absorb some sunshine and star shine. At lunchtime, instead of spending your time with food, walk to some place where you can sit down and let the sun enter into your body, into your thymus. It doesn't matter whether it is a park bench or a chair on a rooftop. When you get home at night, bathe and then go for a walk. When it gets dark, try and find an open place where you can see the night sky. Or go for another walk. You are starving for sunlight and moonlight.

Follow through on this program for a month. After a month you will begin to recover. Your mind will become lighter and brighter. You will be ready to do some exercises. When you establish some discipline with exercise, cut back on heavy food, and continues walking several times a day. You will be ready to meditate. This is the way to get out of the malaise you find yourself in.

Q. **My life is really quite comfortable and my family seems to be going along quite well. There is warmth and affection in the household and my kids are doing well in school and haven't run into any great problems such as drugs, bullying, etc. Still I feel unsatisfied and uneasy about my life.**

A. From the sound of it, it seems as if you have as good a life as anyone could hope for. Still, it is a life. And there is the rub.

Q. **I might be a shopaholic. I go out almost everyday and come home with a new skirt, a new pair of shoes, a new knick-knack, or whatever. I know this is a ridiculous way to spend time and money, both of which I have plenty of, but I don't know how to stop this pattern of behavior or what to substitute it with.**

A. We never get enough of what we don't need.

Q. **Where does happiness come from?**

A. It comes from suffering, just like the Buddha said it did. In the same vein, wisdom comes from stupidity. That should make you feel better!

Q. **Where would we be without Dukkha (Pali for suffering, unsatisfactoriness, and conflict)?**

A. That would be the hell of heaven realm.

Q. **When I think about Dukkha, I think about the states of grief, conflict, pain and death. These kinds of states are awful.**

A. They are awful and they are catalytic, for without Dukkha as the catalyst, one could never reach Nirvana. Suffering is the conduit. When the Buddha directed his discourse toward Dukkha, he was talking about the state of mind that is not abiding in Peace. When we get past the awful states, we transcend time and space and free ourselves from the dreadful states.

Q. **I have to live with a challenging disability. I spend most of my time dealing with this problem, leaving me little time or energy to meditate. Is there a way for me to meditate while dealing with an exact medical regime?**

A. First, recognize that everyone is disabled. I am speaking of mind, not body. The mind is the king from which everything flows out. Those of us with a mind disability stumble around in the dark, all day and all night long. We fumble around under the authority and power of our karma and ignorance. The irony of life is that a pleasant, comfortable, secure condition, the situation we strive for, is the most difficult environment for spiritual growth. Actually, once you close your eyes and turn your attention inward, the energy will come up on its own.

Find twenty or thirty minutes where you can be alone and quiet. Create the meditation habit and I will give you further instructions when you have established a practice.

Q. **Where does real happiness come from?**

A. It comes of its own, out of time, apart from fear, wanting, demanding, imploring, etc. and springs forth uninfluenced, unforced, and unprovoked by desire or worry. We don't know this state of being because the itch of constant anxiety conceals it.

Q. **Some schools of Buddhism assert that practicing solely for ones own Enlightenment is selfish. Do you ever see it that way?**

A. It was a concern I harbored for some years but found that the concern disappears along the Path. By that I mean at first you practice to try and get your head straight, to know who you are not and who or what you might be. Over the years, your Insight resolves these questions and most of your other doubts, concerns and issues that arouse anxiety. As you move along, your practice incorporates more and more of the pandemonium of the world, until, finally and naturally, you practice for your own Enlightenment and for the Enlightenment of all others as well.

Q. **How much of my energy should I spend involved in politics, social issues, environmental issues, etc.?**

A. That's up to you to resolve. What is most important is that you recognize that first and foremost you are a spiritual being. Your priority should be your spiritual development. Then, according to your interest and enthusiasm, you should concern yourself with the areas of challenge which we face living in a society on a fragile planet.

Q. **In your spartan life do you feel some anguish for not having the kind of things you were used to or the kind of things many people have today?**

A. Such as?

Q. **Such as a good pair of shoes, nice smelling soap, TV, DVD, credit cards?**

A. I want less so I have more. The only thing that I want and the only thing missing in my life is the state of ultimate sanity.

Q. So what is our big problem?

A. Fear and its cohort, wanting. We harbor much more fear than we imagine. And that fear chokes our life, cutting off the Happiness that is our birthright. This Happiness is the state of ultimate sanity I just mentioned.

Q. Don't you find that living alone in a cave without TV, radio, or even a cat, to be boring?

A. Living alone or in a group of monks and nuns never feels boring. There is always the sense of seclusion which produces a sense of spiritual stimulation. It's the distractions of the world that bring on boredom. Things that make noise and move around quickly become boring. Silence won't. Silence is invigorating.

Q. Are there various types of Wisdom?

A. Generally, meditators recognize three types of intelligent consciousness. (1). There is wisdom that is arrived at through reflection. This is a process of thinking out. (2). Wisdom can also arise from study. In this case, we learn from others. (3). Then, there is Wisdom arrived at through mental development through meditation practice. At each of these levels insight and wisdom arises. Through the process of reflection, understanding is garnered and views and opinions arise. Study functions in a similar way. However, insight that arises through practice generates a view without anyone holding onto it, a view-less view. Through this mature appreciation of a situation, we transcend clinging to a view, an opinion, a concept or a notion.

Q. **My niece's daughter was born paralyzed and has remained in bed up until today, 12 years later. What did she do to deserve this state of affairs?**

A. That is a situation clearly showing the intertwining karma of parents and children. Her condition, contrary to your sense of it, is not bad. It has created an opportunity to get beyond very heavy karma for both the child and her parents.

Q. **I want to help my kids avoid doing foolish things. What can a mother do to help her kids become mature, stand on their own feet, and live a moral life?**

A. Mothers can only offer guidance to their children. As far as help goes, they can only help themselves. It's enough of a job to help ourselves. To whatever extent we help ourselves, our "beingness" can be a source of encouragement for others. Obviously we can only help others to the extent that we help ourselves.

Q. **One principle I have heard Buddhists speak about is perpetual change. I believe that is called "Annica". As I see it, if everything is in a state of change then there is really nothing at all. Is that the point? Everything is fantasy, everything is dream?**

A. You could say that. But if you clung onto that too hard, every endeavor to broaden and deepen your understanding would seem futile. It is more skillful, I believe, to understand that "Annica" implies that there is nothing within our capacity and capability to control. We simply cannot control things here.

That everything is a dream, that everything is fantasy, is a realization that is profound and not merely a concept. It is not reachable through thought. You can use this as a working hypothesis, as a remedy against your entrenched belief system. If you use this in this way, you can live your life with some recognition that everything may well be a dream. And that, ironically, is reality!

Q. **How deep is ignorance?**

A. That's quite a question! Ignorance is infinite because it involves itself with the defilements. The defilements have no limits for spawning reckless folly.

Q. **I have a friend who has nothing but problems. All his activities seem to lead to more and more problems. The things he gets into are far beyond my ability to resolve. This guy is an ordinary person with a very ordinary background. Why is his life so complex?**

A. Some people have a combination of very heavy karma along with an inclination to make imprudent, bad decisions. Everything that happens in their life gets scrambled. That's all that can be said about it.

Q. As I get older I find myself losing more and more things. The way I deal with this problem is to keep buying more pens, more eye glasses, more keys, etc. Is there a way, at my age, where I can train my mind to remember where I put things?

A. The strategy that you chose to deal with losing things won't get you anywhere. You already know that. You just keep on losing the same things over and over again. *Attention* is the factor you need to develop. Pay attention to the things you use before you move them or before you make use of them. Note where they are. When you finish with them note where you put them. *And be aware of the noting.* Pay attention to where you hands and feet are as you move around your home. Pay attention to the things that arise in your field of vision. Pay attention to the feel of things when you touch them. As you touch and note you evoke memory. As you pay *more attention* to details, to the feel of things, to the arising of objects in your field of vision, the problem of forgetfulness will diminish significantly.

Q. I have chosen to do martial arts and yoga to develop my spiritual side. Perhaps, someday I will be more attracted to meditation. In the meantime, yoga and karate will build up confidence and strength in my body and mind.

A. I don't know if you are about to come to a question or not. Nonetheless let me plant a seed for your contemplation. The qualities attained through meditation practice will ensure that in times of emergency and at the time of your death, your mind will be centered and calm. Because your mind is awake, at peace, and unafraid, your poised-disposition will meet any and all situations with uncommon common sense. You're doing fine.

Q. Apart from a few seconds every blue moon, I don't know if I have really ever established my mind in the present. The present doesn't seem to be the place to be if I want to control things and have some sense of security in my life.

A. This is a tug of war between concern for the future and various emotions concerning the records of the past. When all you know is the past and future, which, by the way, is really the same thing, I suggest that being in the present is the best place to assure security and control. That doesn't mean that your life will be secure or that you will *really* be in control. But it does mean that you won't be overwhelmed by events.

Q. I'm afraid if I put my attention on some invisible mantra within me, my work will fall apart.

A. Actually, if you maintain awareness on your mind, holding it to a skillful meditation object, your efficiency will increase exponentially. Not only will the quality of your endeavors improve but you will soon find you make fewer mistakes, spend significantly less time in doubt and hesitation, and finally, allow more creativity to flow through your life.

Q. I was lonely having broken up with my ex-boy friend two years ago. I met a man I knew years ago that I had always taken a fancy to and within 3 nights I was pregnant with his baby. Of course, everything fell apart and I had the baby on my own. How does this long shot accident happen to so many women?

A. When you combine loneliness with karma, the chances of producing a baby are increased significantly. Loneliness seems to call forth disembodied beings and those waiting to take birth. Out-of-the-ordinary warm and fuzzy feelings which strangely attract us towards other beings indicates a blend of karmic history, for sure.

But even if you weren't lonely, the forces that pull us into unforeseen situations might well have brought both of you together with the same result. This can only be attributed to karma.

Q. After kicking around on this planet for almost 50 years, I have come to the conclusion that I should just do my thing, find some happiness in life, get ancient and retarded and die. While waiting for the golden years I feel I am entitled to indulge in fast foods, fast motorcycles, and weekends in Vegas.

A. I don't see how you can get much satisfaction out of life with that formula shaping your behavior. The buzz words these days are entertainment, fun, play, holiday, fresh and the like. Have you ever contemplated the inevitable cycle involved in these forms of activity? Or, when you pop into a fast food entertainment center and select something from a cleverly designed menu of tempting and enticing fast foods, did you ever notice how they are presented in a way that excites hope? Yet somehow, the entertainment, the excitement, the games, the holidays all fade out and slip into the past, leaving behind nothing but a memory.

On the other hand, have you ever noticed that when you do something difficult, something for others, when you sacrifice your time, sacrifice your laziness, you always get back something of substance, something that doesn't just sink into the unknown and get blown away by the sands of time?

I spend a lot of time everyday engaged in walking and sitting meditation. Much of the time I don't like doing it, but I always like what it does for me.

Q.   **I can now see that mindfulness-awareness or what you call "Sati" provides me with another point of reference, another dimension. That is certainly useful and I am grateful for your help in guiding me into that function. Can you tell me if there are other secondary aspects to this aspect of consciousness?**

A.   There are other benefits that come with touching "Sati" but I wouldn't call them secondary. "Sati" puts us in touch with the rhythms and timing of life. With "Sati", we know the right time to retreat, the right time to be active, the right time to contemplate, and the right time to serve.

Q. **What is karma? And is it something that is always bad?**

A. What if you were to sit in any empty room with a notebook and pen and jot down a note, scribble a drawing? Sounds innocent enough. That innocent gesture connects to all the other actions you have ever taken through the course of your innumerable lives. The world is run on karma. It began with karma and is sustained by karma. Nothing is paying attention: the karma machine manages every relationship between everyone and everything.

Q. **I thought it was love that made the world go round.**

A. That is likely to be just your hope. In reality, love is what puts the crazy spin on that which is going around, namely, karma.

Q. **I have a lot of questions concerning karma, can I hurl a few more your way?**

A. No matter how many questions you pose, there will be many times more you could ask. There is no end to the question of karma. If we are wise, we will just come to understand the principles and then live by them. That is what the wise do.

Q. **Where does the world begin?**

A. It begins with karma. Don't ask me what it was that was the catalyst for the karma, for if you do, I will tell you that karma is its own catalyst. Hearing that won't make you happy.

Finally, kindly realize that karma started your world. Eradicating or deactivating karma sets you free. Most people don't want to be free so they tumble around in the karmic washing machine. Birth, aging, illness, and death. This is the karmic washing machine. The most important question to pursue is how to go about dismantling the momentum of this system. And then, do it.

Q. **But the world will continue whether or not we are here.**

A. Something that is going on and on that doesn't involve you is of no consequence.

Q. **I lived in an Ashram in India for several years. As of the beginning of this year I left the ashram and India and picked up pretty much where I left off. I thought that my simple, celibate years would protect me from my worst habits forever. But actually, it was only a matter of weeks before I became re-accustomed to the patterns of lay life.**

A. Don't underestimate the change that occurred from your time in India. Old habits die harder than you would think. Once under familiar influences, it is easy to slip into the same patterns of behavior. But when you do, your deepened awareness will quickly pull you out, or, at least, make you feel uneasy. You think you returned to the same place, so that when similar situations occur you tend to feel somewhat hopeless and defenseless. This deception makes you think that your time in India was wasted. Not so. Definitely not so. Get over the shock and disappointment. You haven't returned the same. Now your awareness can see the situation, the dangers, and the pitfalls.

Do your duty in the situations you find yourself in. Take care of your mind so that it can be aware of things in a deep and circumspect manner. Maintain your spiritual practices. This is a good opportunity for you to see the power of old habits. Once you pass through this stage, you will be a very strong and mature person in your personal world. Ultimately, you will be affecting a lot of people in the so-called real world in a Good way.

Q. In this age of information I feel it's necessary to continue my studies in order to stay with the fast changing developments. If I were to, say, enter a good monastery and practice meditation for even 3-4 months I suspect the ship will have moved on and I'd be left standing at the dock. Also, to confide my concerns, honestly I think I would change in ways that would make it really, really hard for me to reintegrate into the world I now know.

A. It's true that people call this the information age and that the huge quantity of information is escalating into even greater mountains of information every time we blink. A person could ask himself or herself just how much of this tsunami of information is of real value, just as when people watch an inane commercial for some awful snack food, someone that is at least a little awake would question the value of that food-entertainment experience.

Even more than this being a world of information, it is a world of distraction and diversion. Silicon Valley has invented electronic stuff that puts almost everyone on the cutting edge of news and information. The entertainment content moguls have successfully turned people into mush minds, so much so that many don't even have a clue that almost all of it is empty distractions and diversions. These distractions become obstacles to developing insight and to awakening to the-way-things-are.

Q. **This is an age of anxiety and nervousness. I've opted to take a drug to calm me down and control the anxiety that comes with my work. I expect that you would frown on this strategy but, I have to tell you, it works. And because it works I get my work done.**

A. I take it for granted that there is a question in your comment.

You are welcome to choose your own strategies for the sake of efficiency and ease. As you suspect, using the kind of drug you are using generates a great deal of profit for the drug companies and, seemingly, some profit for you. The drug company is always going to do fine. But what about you? Are you sure that, over time, you made a good choice? That the negative aspects won't erase the positive?

I believe that we should look at the cause. What is the root of anxiety and dis-ease? There are several factors but the agitating factor is one's apprehension about the future. Hundreds of studies have shown that meditation reduces anxiety by deepening and expanding awareness and it doesn't cost anything. Anxiety, worry and fear, mental states that bother you terribly, are something that can be overridden when ones understanding is deepened. The only reality is the present. If you were to concern yourself with the present, the future would simply emerge as the present in its own time. In this modality, acute understanding solves the problem naturally.

Q. **When a good Buddhist, a good Christian, a good Muslim dies, will they all meet and go to the same heaven realm?**

A Causes and effects occur according to the principles of Nature. People can identify themselves as they like, they can call themselves whatever they want, evoke spiritual practices in whatever mode and manner they want, yet the overriding principle affecting what they manifest into will always be the cumulative result of their intentional actions while alive.

There are, of course, refined realms of being where happiness and bliss are the norm. This is the heaven you are asking about. It is a disembodied realm so no being in this realm suffers from old age and illness. Still, the beings in this realm are karmic conditions. They will abide in these realms only as long as the heavenly-realm energies supporting this situation persist. A being cannot stay in the heaven realms indefinitely. Eventually, the positive energies supporting existence in this realm will run out and the being will be cast into the human realm where the struggle to purify the mind will continue beneath the ongoing daily struggle for survival and for meaning.

I hope what I am saying draws attention to the most important thing to understand about our existence. That is that all beings are energies. These energies are known as karmic energies. They have a particular spin, discordant, conflicting momentum. They operate with their own impetus. The way these manifest depends solely on our past intentional behavior. Nature has hardwired us into the Law of Karma in order to create situations for karma to work itself out. What we see in this life is karmic energy seeking opportunities to decontaminate itself. If you see people making mistakes, hurting others, living insensitively, committing crimes, and the like, the superior perspective would be to see these actions as the inclination and drift of karma rather than reflective, free actions of people. If this were widely understood in our culture the criminal justice system would certainly see events and situations with a more compassionate heart.

Q. **If a person is callously wronged, can they ever get over the trauma? In order to get on with life, is it necessary for the wrongdoer to apologize to them for their perceived wrong?**

A. When you look for something outside to happen in order to satisfy or appease yourself, you're generating a fantasy that can never happen, for even if you got what you wanted, two hours later a new demand would arise to trouble you further. The strategy that demands satisfaction through someone else's actions or behavior is hopeless. Understand that hopeless means that there is absolutely, utterly no way the desire for righteousness and justice can ever be satisfied. Your job is really to understand the karmic dilemma involved in the human predicament. If the offender is able to arouse a sense of shame and express regret, that indicates a lesson has been learned. Then, he or she can respond with dignity and nobility that is worthy of praise. That's their "boon". However, for you, the so-called offended or wounded person, your job is to come to understand what "offended" is all about. Who or what is it that feels offended? Be very careful not to get caught in self-righteousness. Watch over yourself by penetrating into the feeling of "offended".

Also, you should be aware that holding on metastasizes the problem and makes us feel worse and worse. The benefit is through evolution.

Q.   **How can they move on and what (if anything) does this have to do with their forgiving the transgression?**

A.   One doesn't have to forgive. If you are stuck in righteousness and injustice, how can you forgive anyone? Better to recognize that all humans have weak spots and that all carry karma from the past that will certainly involve other beings whom they will meet in this life. If you see things from this perspective, a deeper, more comprehensive understanding of yourself and others is certain to arise. In this process of spiritually understanding your karmic predicament, the lessons you need to learn from life, the value of suffering, and your attitude towards the difficulties and challenges all of us have to confront will begin to seep into your consciousness. Yesterday's problem, like the disappointment and trauma you occasionally experienced as a child, will slip away to be replaced by circumspect awareness incorporating wisdom and compassion. You will then know beyond doubt that you're on the Path of evolution.

Q.   **Is penance necessary for the person who did wrong to make things right?**

A.   Is this penance to be prescribed by the wronged person? Penance is not the business of someone other than the person wishing to admit and acknowledge past mistakes and to cease to repeat them.

Q.   **What if the wronged person cannot or will not move on and continues to project evil thoughts toward the cheater in the name of their hurt and pain?**

A.   No condition is forever. You will move on when you are ready and have punished yourself enough. One day you will wake up and see that your vicious energies harm you far more than they harm the person you are busy hating. This is a regular question in the marital consultation field which arises in the aftermath of an affair. There are professionals who have techniques for processing this situation. However, I don't think you have to know any more than I have told you. The understanding that the images you tenaciously cling to can be let go of and that your life can move beyond this experience is all you need to rise above this challenge.

Q.   **Although I am still relatively young I feel worn out. Worn out from trying to make relationships work, worn out from trying to find satisfaction in unsatisfactory work, worn out from interactions with my family, and worn out from visiting therapists. I just feel like I need a long rest. And at the same time I feel like that would just put things on "pause".**

A.   Your life experiences, just like all of ours, have been a tapestry of hurts, slights, disappointments, and betrayals. This is the nature of life. As karma unfolds we are challenged to meet the pain and suffering with patience, acceptance and dignity. Nobody escapes from suffering. You deserve compassion and praise for enduring and surviving through difficult emotional and psychological challenges. Now this is your opportunity to radiate kindness and love toward yourself, to open yourself up to spiritual love, to fortify and heal your heart and, ultimately, to send loving kindness into the world. No one is more deserving of your love and compassion than you.

Kindly order one of the many "Metta" (Loving-Kindness) tapes you can easily find on the Internet. Practice with these for 2-3 hours a day. You will soon get a new perspective on life and come to appreciate your life and the opportunity it is offering you to go beyond.

Q. **I have been meditating in the temple for several weeks now and haven't yet seen the results I hoped for. As you know, I read a best seller book that convinced me that if I set my mind right, all the best things I deserve and all the money I need would be drawn to me. I have been maintaining my concentration on being able to manifest this in my life. I wonder if I am doing this right.**

A. That's quite a wish list you set for yourself! Here is what you can do: write a note covering your hopes and wishes and address it to God or Santa Claus or Bill Gates. Place it in an envelope and mail it. Don't forget the stamp. Then go back to your hut and practice only watching your breath. Do this with all the passion and intensity you can muster.

Q. **Then what?**

A. There need not be any, "then what?"

Q. So I just sit in my hut and wait? What if I wait and wait and nothing happens! I don't get what I want, what I need!

A. You are in no way wasting time. You are practicing strengthening your mind, reducing your desires and fears, and allowing the benefits of the practice to lift you out from under your karma.

If someone knocks at your door offering everything you want, just accept and move along with that energy. If no one knocks, you can accept that and be content with the happiness of your enlightened mind.

Q. I envision the defilements or negative energies in mind as little monsters running around with pitch forks causing trouble whenever they can. But, actually, what do the defilements do in the mind?

A. Your images are not all that way off. Putting it in the simplest terms, the defilements are infections which continually bother us to the point that we become slaves of virus-infected thought. The defilements infiltrate the thought process and then the body and speech foolishly spin these thoughts into the melodrama making relationships between people and things. When the defilements contaminate the emotions, the additional heat inflames an already dangerous situation.

Q. **I feel like I have come to meditation too late in life. Do you think I still have time to develop my mind significantly?**

A. Everybody tends to feel as if they have come to meditation very late in the game. That's just the way it feels. Actually, we all come at just the right time. Once one gets a taste of the happiness of a let-go mind they invariably feel some remorse for not having discovered the nature of the-way-things-are earlier. In reality, you have come just at the right time. You have not been ready until now. The idea of sitting with your eyes closed observing the Nature of mind didn't interest you before. Trying to do something when there is no motivation, especially in regards to meditation, doesn't go anywhere. You might contemplate where the motivation to enter spiritual practice comes from? It's the recognition that consistent, stable happiness is not available in the world of sense pleasures. That is why we all feel unsatisfactoriness and conflict...or existential suffering.

Q. **I am a layman, a householder. In my role as a parent and a partner in a relationship I don't see how I can possibly develop a consistent, disciplined meditation practice. Am I destined to remain stuck pretty much where I am now?**

A. I don't think it is all that skillful to see yourself as a "layman" or a "householder". For that matter I don't believe you should even cling to the idea that you are a "man", someone's "son", an employee in your company, or any of the other various conventional roles you play. Personally, I see myself simply as a karmic condition. The name "monk", "recluse", "mendicant", etc. are conventional ways to describe me.

If you recognize yourself as a karmic condition and all that implies, you will certainly muster up an effective meditation practice within any adverse situation. You will work to solve the problem you face with diligence and courage and the way you are obliged to live will not create an insurmountable problem at all.

Q. **In Buddhism there is the concept of "Annata", which as I understand it, means that there is really no one. All the people and the other things of this world are just a kind of fantasy. I don't get that at all. Here we are. Talking. Communicating. Breathing and living. How can there be no one?**

A. There are beings, people and other sentient life. However, nothing here can be controlled. Things go their own way according to karma. Nothing can be maintained in a perpetual status quo. Things are in never-ending change. That is what "Annata" means. Because nothing can hold its ground, everything is in a state of perpetual alteration; we cannot call it real. In terms of *ultimate* reality, there is no one, no where.

Q. **Sometimes I seem to see things from another kind of awareness. Instantly and without preparation I have a sharper, clearer kind of vision. Is this where meditation takes us?**

A. What you are experiencing we can call intuition. You tapped into an information channel where intuition sees another dimension or a depth that cannot be seen by conventional perception and intelligence. This is enhanced intelligence which is, unfortunately, fragile and fleeting. It arises in a flicker. If it is not caught by an awareness that supersedes conventional wisdom, it disappears immediately and is then engulfed by conventional mentality. Once back to your customary consciousness it is only possible to see the world through one's external senses, experience, personality, hopes and fears.

Q. **I have heard you say and I have read the signs on the big trees that getting up early in the morning is critical to developing meditation. At home, no matter how many times I promise to get up before 5 a.m., I never can do it. Is this a fatal problem?**

A. Not exactly fatal, but certainly dangerous. I am alerting you to a danger that comes from a kind of personal malfeasance. On your previous visit you described your typical day which began at 7:15 am... just in time to jump into your clothes, munch on a donut and rush off to work. Hearing that, I tried to emphasize that the first things you do in the morning set the tone for the whole day, and that the best thing you could do for yourself was to meditate as early in the morning as possible. If you think about it you will be duped into the notion that getting up early will cause you to be tired in the early afternoon. That's not true. Not only will you have more energy throughout the day but your mind will be significantly more lucid. You will make fewer mistakes and get things done more efficiently.

I am willing to repeatedly recommend that you add this experience to your day, but I am not going to stand by your bed at 4:30am to drag you out of your reveries, so it's solely up to you whether you can stimulate yourself to test this out for yourself. The problem of approaching the day in the way that you do is not a fatal fault but it certainly makes you more vulnerable to carelessness and criticism. You won't be able to do much to improve your life without those tranquil early mornings set aside for contemplation and reflection.

Q. **I am part of a group of people who meet together to discuss philosophic inquiry in order to learn about the higher truths. I have been meeting with this group for years. While most nights the things we talk about are interesting and profound, I feel like exploring high-minded ideas is endless. And I wonder where all this will take me. Will my mind become brighter from this practice? Will something stick that will work to produce a good rebirth?**

You may wonder where I am going with this dialogue. I guess I am wondering too! Actually, I really want to know if I am on the right track and if what I am doing is right?

A. What you're doing is right, but it isn't True. What do I mean? Being right means you're not wrong. Investing a lot of time in this pursuit is not wrong. But it isn't True. What do I mean by True? That which is True leads to the Truth. The Truth can only be known from within, experientially. That is, it can only be known through a process that sees things through the prism of Change, unsatisfactoriness, and Non-Self.

One easy way to see the problem is by asking yourself if the data, information, conjecture, ideas etc. which you scrutinize and contemplate enter into you as something personal, i.e. your storehouse of information increases around certain philosophic and spiritual ideas.

Q. **Over the past 40-50 years there have been numerous so-called exposures of various events that reporters and investigators say were conspiracies to hide the truth. I'm thinking about the Kennedy assassination, the events of 9/11, UFO cover-ups, etc. Do you have any insight into what really went on concerning these events?**

A. The only conspiracy I have deemed sufficiently important to study is the one involving the way our societies "educate" and acculturate our mind in order to maintain the fiction about what we really are and what we are here to do. Practicing meditation scrapes off all the propaganda and misinformation that formed our "educated" ideas and ways of thinking. In the end, instead of being a slave of conventional thought patterns, we emerge from that cocoon autonomous, self-reliant, and detached.

As for the theories you mentioned, I wouldn't be surprised if they were accurate.

Q. **I am in a quandary concerning my marriage of 20 years, my job of 23 years and even the value of spending a lot of time with the guys whom I have known and hung around with since high school. My doubts have come to the point where I can hardly sleep. I feel so much energy urging me on towards something else, some life that has more life than the life I am now living. Is this mid-life crisis?**

A. I don't know what "mid-life crisis" is. I expect different experts have different opinions about the sense of meaninglessness you are alluding to.

What I do know about is doubt. You are treading water in a sea of doubt. I suspect you have been doing this for a long time but have only just noticed it. Doubt can be a tricky feeling to deal with. There is the sense of not-knowing at odds with the idea that you should know. When you try to come to a decision, the seeming conviction that you initially embrace slips away from you into the opposing persuasion. And then back again. Doubt has us on a teeter-totter.

Have you ever had the experience of driving to some remote place you have never been to? You have some vague direction so you stop and ask someone and they confirm some of your direction but point you to another road. So you go along that way for some time. When too much doubt arises you stop again and talk to another person who gives you some of the same directions and some new ones. You carry on encumbered with doubt until, finally, the way looks clear. Immediately, doubt disappears and confidence emerges. If you have experienced this situation, you know how well it demonstrates clearly how painful doubt can be. It also demonstrates how confidence, borne out of knowing and the wisdom associated with it, effectively replaces doubt and eradicates suffering. If you practice to see and catch doubt you can induce the antidote, confidence, and this will lead to knowing what to do. Crises in our life come along all the time. We need confidence and wisdom to choose intelligently the way to go.

Q. **I became an expert in a particular species of ants. It has given me the opportunity to travel, speak to and educate people about the need to maintain the natural harmony in Nature.**

A. There are interesting and fascinating things to study and do all over the planet.

Still, we have to honestly ask ourselves just how much meaning our work, our lifestyle actually has. Is our work spiritual, is it sacred?

If you incorporate spiritual principles such as the fact of constant change, the fact of conflict and the fact of nothing being as it seems, your study of ants, or someone's stamp collecting hobby, can be a doorway to a deeper and more profound understanding of life and our personal predicament.

Q. **Will the power of practice either eradicate negativity or keep it suppressed indefinitely through the power of Light-Wisdom-Compassion?**

A. Fascinating question. Not indefinitely, forever. Eradicate? How could one know if that is what occurs?

Q. **I have a big problem with the notion that there is nothing but suffering. I am confident that there is pleasure and that there is happiness intertwined with suffering.**

A. Depends on where you look from. If you consider that every living entity, once born, without exception, inclines toward old age, sickness, and death. These conditions of old age, illness and death encompass so much suffering that we can say the earlier happiness is insignificant or, at least, peripheral. Technically, there is pleasure and there is happiness. However, following another argument we could say that there is nothing but suffering since the unsatisfactory factor is forever present *even* when we are enthralled in bliss. As soon as the factors that manifest pleasure or happiness dissipate, we immediately become distressed to some degree.

Q.   Is the time we live here predestined? I am thinking about people who live out their normal life span. Some people appear to be physically very strong and others physically very weak. Is it true to assume that people born without a great deal of strength and vigor will die before those with a strong physical presence?

A.   I gather you mean does our karma play a part in how long we can live. Certainly. As you said, people who are physically strong can live longer in this hostile environment. But the quantity of life is not so important. It is the quality. Those with the karmic energy to develop wisdom and compassion have a lot more going for themselves than Mr. Universe, Superman, and Spiderman.

Our life force is invariably ticking towards the end of this birth into death. There is a maximum time we can live here. And that maximum time will always involve our karma and our "boon". For me, that fact has generated a sense of urgency.

Q.   What is it that keeps this body and mind together?

A.   We can just call it the "value of life", the factor that brings value to existence. Without this factor, the mind and body would be nothing but machinery.

Q.   What is the cause of suffering?

A.   Responding inappropriately to the moment.

Q. I have always chased after happiness, but what you are saying has made me think about what happiness actually is. I haven't figured this out yet. But a question has come up in my mind concerning the variations of happiness. Different people go after different kinds of happiness flavors. In the end, supposing they get what they want, is the experience the same?

A. In this world there are many varieties of happiness and many gradations of happiness. Consider these examples. Undoubtedly you have seen people who are happy with a cigarette and a bottle of cheap wine, just as you probably have seen, at least in the movies, people that are happy with a cigar and a bottle of expensive wine. Here, what causes happiness depends upon some external factor. People reach out for the taste of happiness in both gross and refined variations. Just contrast watching birds with hunting elephants. From the sensual and sexual to the macabre. The world offers a whole range of means to experience happiness allowing people to reach for the kind that suits their character and karmic proclivities.

Then, there is the happiness that is above the world, above the senses. A superior Happiness that comes out of developing and maintaining awareness. A happiness that doesn't depend on anything whatsoever in the world. It is the happiness that comes from a peaceful mind: a mind that doesn't want anything, that isn't anxious, that sees clearly what-is-what and what is Good.

Q. I have a teenage son and daughter. They seem to be doing all right in school. Hopefully they will go on to college. Their grades are good enough and, so far, they have kept out of any big trouble. We have a fund to pay for their education.

Still, I fret about what will become of them. They don't have any special talents and their IQ is in the ordinary range. What can a parent do to help their kids?

A. I can understand your anxiety. 99% of the kids I have seen who have graduated with one degree or another hardly seems equipped to deal with life. While they may have an ornate paper that provides them with the opportunity to find a suitable white collar job, they are sadly ill equipped to deal with disappointment, doubt, illness, anticipation, praise/blame, jealousy, etc. Few know the factors necessary to build good, strong relationships, as well as the elements and behavior patterns that destroy relationships. These are the real pedestrian challenges that our lives have to tackle.

Since you are here talking with a monk, I recognize that your concern isn't about their academic endeavors. What you want to know is what can a parent do to help them avoid heartbreak and despair? The first thing to recognize and keep in mind is that your children are karmic conditions. That is, they have taken birth impacted with the positive and negative energies that were produced from earlier intentional actions. From the time of birth, a child is impacted with influences from the culture, the school, the state religion, and the family. These factors are mostly out of your control. Your child is really more a child of all these influences than he/she is yours.

The child will proceed through life with all these influences (and more added over time) affecting their behavior, activities, and decisions. You have very little power to do anything more than advise and guide.

Your advice and guidance could be critical. Kindly recognize the impact of your own personal habits and behavior. If they see you as a role model, you really don't need to talk all that much. However, if there are serious defects in your personal behavior, there won't be all that much opportunity to offer advice and guidance. The die has been cast.

From this point in time and space, try and incline your life more and more towards the spiritual quest. You will do the best you can for yourself and your efforts will have a profound effect on your family and friends.

Q.   **Six months ago my marriage fell apart. Since that time I have been feeling confused and lonely. Actually, lonelier and lonelier. My brain is telling me that this is natural. We humans are gregarious social creatures. But there is something else in my mind suggesting that being alone is o.k. Can you tell me something I don't know about these energies?**

A.   If we look closely we can see that that societies have come to exalt family and family-like relationships. Because of that partiality, other life-styles are seen as a threat or even as heresy. For example, in the case of monks and nuns who seek to live alone even while in community, the world sees them as somewhat of a joke, odd people who have been unable to fit into a family structure.

This is actually part of a conspiracy against alone-ness. Aloneness is not a plight. However, modern societies collude both to create social cohesion in order to bond people together and to divert people's minds away from understanding much about the human predicament. When people are identified as consumers, as workers, as mothers and fathers, etc. it is easy to manipulate and control them. As I understand it, this is a facet of the science of social engineering. Most people live their whole lives dependent upon others and addicted to the need for group approval.

I don't know where the word "alone" comes from but I suspect it comes from "all-one". All one as in wholly one. Or, holy one! Regardless of the derivation of the word, the important thing to understand is that aloneness is a skillful state of being. It implies quiet, introspection, meditation and contemplation. It is the most beneficial status possible to be able to reflect on one's life, one's karma, one's duties, one's responsibilities, and one's opportunities. In embracing aloneness we identify ourselves as, primarily, spiritual beings. If I were you I would cherish this opportunity life has given you. No doubt you mourned the end of your marriage. That is a necessary step in the healing. After closing that phase of your life it is now time that you move further along by making use of the kind of solitude that you have in your life. Most people hurry to fill the so-called vacuum with more new distractions. You can do that. But I would recommend that you accept and cultivate the aloneness for some time. If you do, you will benefit greatly.

Q. **I live a busy life that keeps me on the go from dawn to dusk. How can I use my situation to understand Buddhism in a deeper way?**

A. It sounds like your lifestyle is incompatible with spiritual development. No situation is hopeless. However, thought can intervene and crush your confidence. Everyone can work and try to maintain awareness in the present. That alone is a corridor for inner development. It would be best if you could prioritize your interest in spiritual development. If you see it as just some small aspect of your busy life, not much will happen. Spiritual development needs nurturing. For instance, when you first wake in the morning, if you read or listen to aspects of the Buddha's Teachings you can take that Teaching with you all day and reflect upon it. You will find that you have many, many moments when you can wholeheartedly bring your attention to your teaching for the day. Attending to the Buddha's Teaching in this way will add another dimension to the flow of events that punctuate your life. Sometimes, exactly the concept you are contemplating will "work" in a situation that has arisen in your life.

Also, before you go to sleep, you can turn your attention to a facet of the Teaching. You will sleep better and, sometimes, awaken with an image or symbol associated with what you read before closing out the day. If you maintain this kind of discipline, you won't feel disempowered by your hectic life.

Q. **I think I must have a very short attention span because when I listen to Dharma talk I find that I can only pick up on a few points. Is there is a way to listen which will help me listen with more continuity and focus?**

A. Don't make a problem out of this. Actually, everyone hears what they need to hear, what they are ready to hear, and that which resonates with their character. Some things that you listen to but cannot hear will, over time, transform from impenetrable to transparent. A Dharma talk is a refined exposition concerning matters of great importance. Because of the nature of Buddha-Dharma, we must listen carefully. Listening carefully and with focus requires considerable energy. It is almost impossible to catch everything contained in a good Dharma talk. As I said a moment ago, you are hearing what is appropriate for you, at a particular time, concerning your karma and situation.

Q. How long will it take for me to reach Nibbana?

A. Ask me how long it takes to travel a distance of 40 miles.

Q. How long does it take to go 40 miles?

A. It depends upon how fast you go.

Q. Why does the feeling of sadness wash over me? It just comes out of nowhere and in a split second tears flow out of my eyes.

A. We feel sad because we were born.

Q. When I look around at this world, to use a much overused word, I am simply amazed. The whole thing is a mystery that humbles me. I think seeing things in this way is a spiritual practice as well.

A. Yes, the world is an amazing something. I, too, feel awe and humility. Still, our part, why we are here, what there is for us to do, what dangers challenge us, and where we can find help are critical and much more skillful standpoints. We need to solve the problem of birth and death which is at the heart of the legacy of our inheritance called karma.

So, regardless of whether the Universe is amazing, awe-inspiring, or utterly incredible, our personal dilemma remains the same. We must rise above the negative energies that have tremendous power and authority over our behavior and pull ourselves out from under the influence of our karma. If we do, the nature of the world will no longer have any meaning for us.

Q. **How does "Sati" (mindfulness-awareness) deal with vagrant thoughts?**

A. As you know, unless the mind has reached Samadhti, thought just doesn't stop.

"Sati" protects us from being sucked into thought, thereby enabling us to observe life. We don't have to be caught by the passing thought parade. We can see thought and have perspective so that thought can be seen as an object rather than an injunction to initiate behavior. Even more importantly as a protector, "sati" keeps us from following emotions which can drag us into vicious, ugly, unbecoming behavior. The jails are full of people who allowed passionate emotions to dictate their behavior. So, the benefit of "Sati" is incalculable.

Q. **I have been volunteering to visit inmates in the prison near to my home. I have been doing this for three years and have been becoming more and more depressed with every visit. Like my friends, I had hoped to see the prison system put more resources and interest in helping prisoners rehabilitate themselves. However, from what I have seen, everything has remained the same with prisoners, for the most part, locked up in cages until their time is up. The authorities are opposed to our offer to teach meditation or even positive thinking amongst the prisoners. Therefore, we spend most**

of our time with bureaucratic paperwork. Do you have any suggestions on how we can improve the situation? If the value of meditation were better understood the prison system bureaucrats would surely want to initiate programs that would serve the prisoners as well as the State.

A.   You're facing the problem of how to help the world. Your sensitivity and compassion is certain to cause you a lot of suffering. The prison system is punishing you, as well. When there is empathy and compassion but relatively little wisdom, all attempts to improve the world will meet with frustration and a sense of futility.

First, you must understand the nature of the world and its institutions. What are the core aspects of the world? Pain, suffering, conflict, power, greed, lack of compassion, and ignorance. All of these factors can be seen in Darfur, Rwanda, the Balkans conflict, the Holocaust, all the wars past and present, and, most shamelessly, in every instance of the many attempts to exterminate an entire ethnic group or tribe.

This is the world, my friend. Know it for what it is. If you know the world for what it is, you will avoid a considerable amount of frustration and futility. When I say the world is like that, I mean it is like the color red, or the color green. They are what they are and there is no way they can be anything else. We can change the variation of these colors but we can't change the colors.

It is possible to make small adjustments in the way the prison system operates, but you can be sure that the main intention of the prison authorities is to keep people securely locked up for as long as possible. Keeping them in a cell is the easiest and safest way to do that. Retribution and punishment are the ways of the world. Compassion, concern for human rights, rehabilitation and the like are energies above the world and, therefore, have only a modest impact here. You need to get your aspiration in line with the-way-things-are.

Q. **Like my friend I have attempted to do social work but always found that I was too sensitive and too compassionate to do much good. I only get caught in frustration and disappointment.**

A. I don't think we can be too sensitive or too compassionate. Where we fail is in not joining these worthy energies with wisdom. Then, we can see what is appropriate, what can be done and what can't be done. There won't be frustration or disappointment if we understand the situation properly.

Q. **I have noticed that whenever I follow my intuition, it is right more often than when I follow my thoughts. I find that a little spooky. Why is that?**

A. People dismiss their intuition because it doesn't seem to connect to anything. In fact, it represents innate wisdom. This energy is energy not associated with experiences or rationality. It usually gets overruled by indoctrinated, conventional rationality.

Q. Rarely can I find the time to meditate. If I manage to find time, when would be the best time to sit?

A. Anytime is a good, skillful time. Any time is all time.

Q. What is the difference between pleasure and Happiness?

A. Happiness is a mode of being. Pleasure is a momentary pain-free incident which occurs in the flow of time. It's good you wish to differentiate them. Pleasure has become a commodity which is marketed and sold worldwide. Happiness is not something we can buy. It doesn't arise by going after it. It does not come out of anything we pursue as in the "pursuit of Happiness". As a result, Happiness couldn't ever get a 15-second slot on a late night game show. For us to understand and realize this Happiness requires determination and hard work. Few people ever taste it.

Q. I am a fashion designer. I have worked with many of the famous people in the business. Most of the time, I work with fabrics, trying to create something new and exciting. Ninety nine per cent of the time nothing much comes together in a way that pleases me. However, every once in a while something wonderful does happen and in that rush of creativity something magical happens. To be utterly candid, that's the only time in my life I really feel delighted and alive. These now-and-again episodes are what I call my "creativity whirlwind." When I am in that energy I don't feel any of the dissatisfaction of life which Buddhists point to. Is creativity the way to escape suffering?

A. When you are in that "creativity whirlwind", your attention is on riding the high. You don't see that the energy push or the energy rush is impacted with tension and anxiety. For the most part, this kind of creativity is actually painful, only you do everything you can to avoid seeing that aspect. This is creativity with suffering. You love the few moments of inspiration when creativity is flowing freely. Apart from those brief moments, there is frustration, anxiety, and disappointment. There is creativity that is spontaneous and doesn't involve the self at all *This is creativity without suffering.* It is a spurt of energy similar to "The Zone" that baseball players speak about or basketball players love so much.

Q. **Sometimes I feel like I'm just keeping above water, treading for survival. I have to pay attention to things and respond in a good way or things will get worse. Other times everything is o.k. and I sort of fall asleep in my life. I don't know which is worse.**

A. There are times when we need to consolidate our energies. Sometimes life flows easily. When things flow easily, there is synchronicity. When there is synchronicity it's time to grow. When things are in harmony you feel at ease and safe. That's the time to scroll down. Don't lose sight of the fact that nothing is permanent. This is the most important thing for you to keep in your mind. What you are talking about illustrates how adversity magnetizes our complete attention and, therefore, is more useful in our life than comfort and security. It's ironic how we struggle to get ourselves into the comfort zone (i.e. spiritual death-mode), relinquishing the opportunities to grow through adversity. By the way, which of these situations do you want to prevail? And why? Wouldn't it be more pragmatic to change your attitude towards the difficulties you face, for you to see them as a challenge and as an opportunity to progress?

Q.   **I feel as if I have been tricked into spending much of my life chasing after, really, nothing of consequence.**

A.   Excellent observation. You have seen through the stuff that obscures the Reality. I expect you are talking about the emptiness of most jobs and careers the world inclines us towards. However, if you look clearly, you will see that the conventional educational system is intended, essentially, to help you find a job after matriculating. Within that system there is very, very little of substance. Education sucks. The products advertisers scream at us to buy are not very good for us. The medicines the doctors provide tend to expand our illnesses. Most of the food on the shelves of supermarkets destroys health. They are packaged well, convenient to prepare, and void of organic nutrition. The rice and bread that we eat is not the same vitamin-rich food our ancestors ate. The bottled water we have to rely on is wet enough but has lost all its life force. All governments waste money on frivolous, foolish, and crony-prone expenditures. All the pandemic illnesses such as cancer, heart disease, kidney disease, etc. originate from malnutrition, stress, pollution, and profit-based science. Cars, even the most expensive, fail safety tests. Building materials, ten years after their initial development, prove to be toxic. Clear cutting the forests for development steals vital oxygen, etc. So, if we can't believe in, rely on, or have faith in the world, where can we turn with confidence towards something of real value? When you come to this question, you have arrived at the starting gate. Now, you can move on into spheres of interest of real significance.

Q.   I have an uncomfortable nagging sense that I am now on the third round of the same old thing. Romance, marriage, family, house, mortgage, new car, car payments, etc. De'jÉvu ? Moving from city to city has not changed this syndrome. My life continues to repeat itself. Are we on a merry-go-round?

A.   This is not De'jÉvu. It's the way things are. The merry-go-round will whirl around as long as we cling to the pole. Life will repeat the same thing if we don't upgrade our perspective and take intelligent and intuitive risks to break out of the patterns we get caught in. Certainly, as you are experiencing, everything will continue to go round and round as in a fishbowl. Observe the international news and you see how governments continue to do the same things, make the same mistakes, etc. America in Vietnam, in Iraq, in Afghanistan, the British in America, India, Africa, Israelis and Palestinians, movie stars with serial marriages, and the Russians in the Balkans. The principle is that the powerful countries will try and eat up their vulnerable neighbors. You shouldn't need to ask a Buddhist monk about The-Wheel-Of-Life as the repetitive pattern of things is self-evident.

Q. **I don't know who the good guys are anymore. Some of the people I thought were good, once they got power became bad.**

A. The line between good and bad becomes more and more blurry as the interactions between countries (politics), religions, technologies, etc. gets more and more murky. That is why it is all the more important to be able to come to the place where wisdom resides and allow wisdom to determine the choices and direction of your life. Then you are free of looking outside yourself for direction.

Q. **I am seeing how much doubt I have in my life and how much anxiety it is causing me. Still, I doubt that I can do anything about it!**

A. May I relate to you the story of doubt? This doubt thing is quite insidious. And it is omnipresent in most people's lives. For example, suppose you are in an ice cream shop and you need to make a simple decision between vanilla or chocolate ice cream. No doubt you are a little excited about the prospect of eating some of Ben and Jerry's finest in just a matter of minutes. All you have to do is decide between vanilla or chocolate, both being long time favorites. Looking back, we can see that when the desire for ice cream initially became aroused, it gripped your attention, directed your feet toward the ice cream shop and now here you are standing in front of the lady patiently holding the magic scoop. You should be happy but what you are experiencing is bewilderment. Vanilla or chocolate? To vanilla or not to vanilla? To chocolate or not to chocolate? Some of each will definitely not satisfy.

What is happening in the mind? What is happening is that in one moment a decision is made for vanilla. But in the next moment a new decision overrides vanilla and chocolate wins. Then, in the next moment, vanilla regains supremacy. And so it goes. The net effect is suffering, for the nature of doubt is to oscillate without ever settling once and for all upon one thing. Its decision-making power is so weak that it can "never make up its mind." This situation will not be resolved until the doubter gives up trying to have things both ways and refuses to allow the mind to continue with this maddening process. The doubter overrides doubt and comes down on one side or the other resolutely. It takes firm and adamant energy to escape from doubt.

This situation would be humorous if it didn't take command of so many people's minds. Doubt is a mental disease that comes about from allowing the mind to weaken to the point that doubt can, in fact, torture us even when we are confronted with the most mundane and self-evident circumstances.

Q.   **Is the soul in the body or in the mind?**

A.   Neither. The soul is neither in the body nor in the mind. It isn't anywhere because it doesn't exist. It exists only as a concept in our mind to try and secure continuity, to try and establish ourselves as an enduring entity. In reality, there isn't anything of substance anywhere at all. The concept of soul arises out of hope and confusion.

It disappears once we investigate and find nothing of substance in a sea of ever-changing phenomena arising and passing away. When we see this situation with clarity and wisdom, the fear factor that generates the concept of soul is displaced with awareness of the insubstantiality of everything. Then, a new, distinct kind of sense of security arises that cannot be described; it can only be known. With this security comes the assurance that all is well and that our inability and incapacity to be the owner of anything whatsoever is quite all right.

Q. **I hear my president talk about helping people in other countries attain freedom. I live in a country that professes to be free and I can tell you without hesitation, I certainly don't feel free at all.**

A. How can you feel free when you are tormented by negative energies? When, from the time you get up to the time you go to sleep, you are constantly being pulled about by unsatisfactoriness, conflict, doubt, anger, lust, fear, etc.? I wouldn't pay much attention to the distorted definitions politicians create. Real freedom is freedom from negative energies. Real freedom comes from escaping from harmful influences such as greed, anger, and foolishness. When anyone is under the power of anger or greed, can there be any doubt that they are a slave of hurtful and toxic energies? If we talk about the problems that come from following foolish thoughts, we'd be enumerating the varieties of problems well into the next century. Why not elect some people who are committed to increasing the GNH-Gross national happiness?

Q. **I try, really try hard to discipline my eating habits, my**

drinking habits, my sleeping habits and all my other habits. But, for the most part, I fail. Some disgusting habits seem to stop on their own. I can't take any credit for that. Most persist. Am I destined to live like this until I die?

A.   Some behavior patterns peter out over a short span of time. Others will persist and demand confrontation. The ones that just stop tempting you to act foolish have shallow roots. The ones that have you dancing on a string for years, for decades are much more deeply rooted. Everyone's karma is different. Things that make trouble for you won't bother someone else. And vice versa. Everyone born on this planet is under the authority of these energies; only the dance is different. We are all obliged to free ourselves from their domination. That's the primary reason we take birth.

Q.   **Recently I had a two hour consultation with a psychotherapist. He recommended that I take some pills to control my depression. I bought them but kept them in my medicine cabinet for some weeks before I took two of them. Just last week I felt overwhelmed with acute depression so I took them to help me get to sleep.**

A.   I suppose there is something inside us that would like to get a lifetime prescription for some pill that would keep sadness and depression far away, allowing us to cuddle up into peace and serenity, a magic pill that made us feel like "everything is o.k. dear, mummy is looking after you". However, the best the pharmaceutical industry has been able to come up with are pills that flatten out emotions, dull the response mechanisms and put people to sleep. We don't need to dwell on the dangerous adverse effects that are inherent in all these medicines. The worst side effect is the psychological addiction that comes with depending on anything outside of us. One major side effect of pill medicines is the fear of its withdrawal. That condition itself implies addiction. Instead of subduing the distress, we end up augmenting the situation with addiction and dependence. Pills only benefit the pharmaceutical companies. They make the companies very happy for they produce lots of digits at the bottom line. They have become the biggest industry in the world. Millions of people are addicted to mood drugs (so called anti-depressants). Is the world a depressing place? Look around. It all depends how we see things. If we could see things clearly we would recognize that this world is designed to help beings resolve their karma. The lives we live are the lives we need to live. The difficulties and conflicts that we encounter are the fodder that develops our understanding of the-way-things-are. That is how we evolve. When you come to understand who you are, why you are here, and what needs to be done, you won't think about dis-empowering yourself with medicine. The medicine you will honor will be the medicine that deepens your understanding and expands your perspective.

Q. **I don't know if you would call me schizophrenic or something similar, because I have begun to notice that there are times when I feel a lot of happiness, followed by times when I feel down and depressed. There seems to be no middle ground.**

A. If you observe more carefully you will find that there is lots of middle ground. In fact, most of your experiences fall into a neutral mode, a colorless, nonchalant kind of experience. This kind of experience is pervasive, you just haven't noticed it. It's true that when there is spirited exhilaration brought on by delight you are going to feel happy. It can have a dazzling impact upon your consciousness. However, this happiness is fragile and destined to pass quickly. And, because happiness arises out of various conditions, unhappiness will certainly emerge to take its place. That's Law. Unhappiness is the other side of happiness. If you are attached to wanting only happiness, the inevitable change will bite hard.

I can tell that you have been focusing on these two modes exclusively, that's why you don't see that most of life is neither happy nor unhappy. If there were only these two options we would all be schizophrenic! Begin to pay more attention to the nondescript ordinary state. You will discover that observing the passing flow of life, though not exciting, is serene and brings with it a quality of contentment that is greater than the struggle for happiness and its companion, unhappiness.

Q.   **I have been meditating everyday now for three months. Up until last week I really didn't see much happening. Even though I didn't see anything developing or unfolding, I kept on with it because I made a New Year's resolution to give meditation a try this year. Last week, as I toiled on day after day with more and more doubt I was surprised to experience something amazing. I still don't know what to make of it. I had been sitting quickly trying to maintain a connection to the mantra you gave me when all of a sudden I had a sense that the floor under me had opened and I was falling into an unknown world. I was shocked and scared. But, somehow I had enough faith to feel that whatever was happening was all right. I wasn't going to die and I wasn't going to lose my mind. A moment or two later I realized that I no longer felt the weight of my body and most of my thinking disappeared.**

A.   Very good. What you experienced is the mind coming together. You see, the original mind is only one thing. Your practice brought it back to its original state. In its original, undiluted, unadulterated, uncorrupted, and un-scattered state, the mind is able to utilize its full power. It can see things as they are without the distractions that normally blur and obstruct. When that shift occurs, it might feel like the floor dropped out from under you or you might hear the crack of rolling thunder. Other things can manifest, depending on one's character. Regardless of what marks this evolutionary state of being, what you have accomplished will produce a radically different state of mind. Once we savor this experience, there is no going back.

Q. **What exactly is the target of meditation?**

A. That is something you will have to experience for yourself. This will help you. Experiment with this exercise. Take a deep inhalation and hold your breath. Now, look at the mind ground. You will find that thoughts have ceased. What you experience is the other side of thinking, conceptualizing, fantasizing, and reminiscing. We can call this the target of meditation.

Q. **The Chinese communist government invaded Tibet, killed many monks and nuns and installed a Han Chinese government. They seem to be getting away with this form of terrorism. When will they reap the karma of their savage destruction of the Tibetan culture?**

A. Karma unfolds in many ways. Nobody, no government, gets away with anything. That's Law. The results of karma unfold in their own time. I don't think it is even sequential. For instance, the Chinese entered Tibet and have terrorized the population for many decades now. We all know that they have done everything they can to destroy the native culture--imprisoning monks and nuns, displacing the native population with Han Chinese, torturing the elders, seizing property, burning down temples. They picked up terrible karma. Fifty years before this ruthless exploitation and destruction, the Japanese military burst into Nanking mercilessly raping and killing a large percentage of the population. You may think the retribution for attacking Tibet is out of order, out of sequence. I don't. While the factors of karma are many and varied, it may be that historical time does not determine when our debts must be paid. What is certain is that they *must* be paid.

Q. **I have heard from other teachers, in other traditions, whom I have stayed with that discipline is a prerequisite for spiritual development. Apart from staying on a diet for a few weeks, I have really not attempted to control my behavior. I just try to avoid going over the top. If it's so important, how can I develop discipline and in what areas of my life should this discipline be focused?**

A. I know this sounds fuddy-duddy and out-of-date but we all need to establish ourselves in moral and ethical discipline before doing anything, particularly meditation. Everyone has to start from where they are. Don't harass yourself, as some people do, into thinking that you might be too flawed to turn yourself around. Your old behavior, your old standards are the past. The past is only a memory.

At this juncture in your life, you are intent on inclining your life towards more refined behavior, more refined attitudes. Take one of the five precepts, such as not killing, and make that the pillar of your discipline. Determine that you will not kill anything. This certainly includes cockroaches and mosquitoes, along with everything else that has the sentient life force. That should be easy.

But to hold to this precept impeccably requires vigilance. You don't want to be seeking vengeance on mosquitoes.

This is the first step, the most fundamental of the moral restraints. Then, two or three months later, you can determine to refrain from taking anything whatsoever that doesn't belong to you. This is the precept that prohibits stealing. When you determine to adhere to your vow you will find that life presents all kinds of situations where this precept comes into play. This precept, as well as the other three, requires vigilance as well.

Please don't hold the notion in your mind that there is any kind of instant remedy along the Path of Awakening. Incline more to the notion that all of us have to somehow return back through our characters, our preferences, our bias in order to abide in the original, empty mind. And, having done that, we will come to our natural, original mind.

Q. **If I wanted you to be my teacher, could I just ask you?**

A. I regard myself as a "Samana", someone who is seeking to come to the end of the world. There are supporters of this retreat space who regard me as their teacher. They come to me for guidance and attempt to follow the Path which the Buddha pointed us towards. Obviously, in this teacher-student relationship I have to take a certain amount of responsibility for their well-being and development. That is why I hesitate to accept the designation and role of a teacher.

For some mature students who pretty much have their feet on the ground, have set their priorities right, and are not burdened too much by family responsibilities and /or work obligations, a skillful pointing toward a blind spot, at the right time and in the right way, can save them several lifetimes. In these cases I am delighted to offer assistance and encouragement to facilitate their progress. However, someone might wish to have a teacher just as they might wish for an "iphone" or an MP5 player, while the highest priority in their life is to continue lying on the beach drinking beer! The answer to your question is, "it all depends."

Q. **I have been practicing yoga for over 10 years while studying Hinduism. The books I have studied all teach that "All is One", that we are really just one thing and that we already possess all spiritual knowledge. I recognize that this is true because it rings true and makes sense. Still, I can't say that "I get it!"**

A. What you learn from books are just bare ideas. In order to realize the Truth of Principle in this world you can't just start from an idea, decide that it meets your hopes or your model for the way-things-are and go with it. In order to truly understand that "all is one" you must develop the skillful practices that will *take you through* the confusion and ignorance that clouds and distorts your world. And to do that you need to get to the other side of the thought machinery. When you reach the end of thought, the fact that "all is one" will emerge of its own out of pristine clarity, not from belief or idea.

Q. **I still don't understand the difference you make between "real" and "true". Could you elaborate, please?**

A. What does it mean to be true but not Real? It's true that the sun sets in the West. But that's not real. The sun sets in the West relative to this planet.

It's true that strawberry ice cream is better for some people. It's not absolute Reality. It's a "reality" based on concepts. For instance, anyone can say that a particular flavor of ice cream or a particular brand of beer is the only real ice cream, the only real beer. Other flavors, other brands are approximations or imitations. This conclusion is obviously based on someone's biases and preferences. It is a choice that has taken precedence through the workings of the mind (mainly through experience). It is not absolute.

Sitting with one's eyes closed for 10 days observing a particular condition can be called meditation. That's true. However, in line with principle, meditation is not just a sporadic activity performed within a greenhouse environment. Nor is it simply relaxation. Real meditation involves continuous mental development, continuous cultivation of "Vipassana", which is intended to empower the mind. A mind that has been developed through the synergy of discipline (morality), concentration and Insight (Vipassana) can challenge the defilements (even the most fundamental and dangerous ones--lust, greed, ignorance, and anger) and thereby get beyond conflict and unsatisfactoriness (suffering). More than through any other discipline, the radical effect of the genuine Buddhist practice will certainly be seen in the simple, effortless way of life that arises when the ego-thought-driven world is moderated. The meditator is progressing beyond conventional perspectives; his/her actions are appropriate for they come out of wisdom and compassion.

So, I offer this for your contemplation.

Q. **I guess I am a slow learner but now, finally, I can look back on the past twenty years and recognize that I made a lot of poor decisions. My friends don't look all too happy about how their lives have turned out as well. When we are young and inexperienced, I guess we make poor choices that stay with us for a lifetime. Is there any way I can help my teenage kids make better decisions? They have to think about colleges and relationships.**

A. When we don't have the tools or the ability to utilize intelligence, we make defective decisions that become the basis for further faulty decisions down the line. For instance, an unsound, hastily chosen career choice can haunt you over the span of a lifetime. Our work has to match our character. Or, a marriage based on something utterly unreliable like romantic love, money, or convenience will invariably launch huge difficulties down the road. At the very least it will be a weak foundation for rearing children. Then, as any child psychologist can attest, you have created a dysfunctional world of complex problems. Common sense should allow us to see clearly that a contentious, unloving environment is fertile ground for difficult and painful problems to arise. In the post-modern world there are no shortages of dysfunctional families. Without common sense, which is another way of talking about discriminating wisdom, we become serial bad-decision makers.

The way to help your children make better decisions is to encourage them to strengthen their minds through meditation practice. There are no fixed answers to the challenges we face in life. You can't give them an answer book containing the "right" answers for every situation. Decisions have to be made according to the conditions present at a given time. That is why the only thing we can rely upon is mind. Encourage them to meditate.

Q. I believe that I am quite a generous person. There have been many, many times when I just felt like I was giving, giving, giving, while getting almost nothing in return. I expect you will tell me not to expect anything in return for my efforts.

A. You're right. Generosity is a wonderful trait to cultivate. In one of the Buddha's earlier lives he topped the charts in this area by offering his life to a starving lioness so that she could feed her cubs. Don't try to do this in your home! The principle is, give what is appropriate to the situation *and* don't expect anything in return.

Q. Every time I pass a beggar I feel either guilty or angry. Sometimes I feel both: guilty and angry that they exploit my guilt with their sad expressions. Are Buddhists expected to be generous and offer everyone with a hand out money?

A. You're creating a problem where there need not be one. Do this if someone appears to be authentically in need; respectfully put a few coins in their cup. Instead of weighing the evidence concerning their situation and getting caught up in a whole swarm of emotions, just see your gift as an investment. The downside is minimal.

Q. From the time I was a child, scientists have upgraded the age of the Universe by millions and billions of years. Now the numbers are quite tremendous. But, perhaps, not as colossal as they should be. Recently, I read that Buddhas come into this world system over periods of time like thousands of

times greater than the estimated age of the Universe. How can this be?

A. The texts that I am familiar with indicate that Buddhas come into this world very, very, very rarely. How rarely? The result comes out of multiplying 20 epochs by 100,000 infinities. You might say that that order of time is impossible being that it exceeds the age of this world. That may be. The time frame I am talking about is time in heaven realm. There, time is radically different. Don't try to think about it or you will go crazy.

Q. **I have to speak honestly and humbly, I have been meditating for one and a half years and I have yet to see anything happening.**

A. Progress and benefits in meditation don't come sliding down like hamburgers at McDonalds. It's more like the Internet loading with a r-e-a-l slow connection. We get up early in the morning, wash, do some yoga, and then come to the sitting posture, then again in the evening, instead of gazing at the T.V. The practice develops slowly in the same way as it does when we learn a foreign language. I can guarantee you that there is progress happening regardless of whether you see it or not. In a way, you're asking the mind to judge the development of the Heart, something the mind is incapable of doing. Some people develop slowly, others more quickly. Nonetheless, this work needs to be done and I congratulate you on your perseverance and endurance.

Q. I just began to meditate some months ago because my kids have been at it since college. They have been encouraging me for years to try it. Although I am way past middle age, I still want to be in tune with the times. Do senior citizens like me still have time and the brain power to get results?

A. Meditation isn't much a matter of brain power. The significance of the benefits you obtain is determined by the "goodness" you accumulated in the past and the amount of effort you bring to the practice now. Regardless of your age, it is possible for you to become Enlightened within 7 days! It all depends. Perhaps you don't have such high aspirations. But deep within you, as with all of us, there is a commanding desire to understand this life we are obliged to live. Here is where meditation is critical. The search for meaning will begin and end within yourself.

Q. I see you mix all your food in one bowl. Do you find that delicious? When people offer you food and then see it is all poured into your bowl, doesn't that put them off a bit?

A. The villagers here and throughout Thailand know that our bowl represents "the head of the Buddha". They know that we respect their generosity and that all food eaten eventually goes to the same stomach. We just shorten the process a bit. As for concerns about pleasurable tastes, we substitute delicious flavors for interesting combinations.

Q. Most of the time I just feel kind of dull and lethargic. Sometimes I have energy to do things, but even in the rare instances when that happens, I don't get anything done

for the energy quickly dissipates before I can get going. Basically, I don't see the point in doing anything in this life.

A.   If you could see what is at stake you would certainly bring more gusto into your life. This is where wisdom is so critical, for it is wisdom that seeks improvement, seeks to deepen our perspective on life, and to refine our sensitivity to the things and people around us.

It sounds like you don't have quite enough wisdom to get going. Where does wisdom come from? It comes out of nature. That's automatic. What's required is the effort in developing harmlessness followed by the next stage, the development of tranquility. When the mind is at peace, wisdom will arise. As it arises, allow it to lead your life and you will certainly find more happiness, more satisfaction and a sense of fulfillment in every aspect of your life. Vital energy will replace lethargy because you will recognize that your time is limited and there is a lot to do.

Q.   **Is there an easy way for me to understand what happens when someone is Enlightened? I just can't conceive of what that can mean.**

A.   The idea or notion of who you think you are disappears. That's why you can't understand it. You must disappear from the conventional reality to be able to understand Enlightenment. Actually, there is no way to "understand"; it can only be "Realized", "Realized" as in, "to know the Real".

Q. I have studied enough science to recognize the beauty and elegance of the universe. If we look at the world as a place of suffering, we completely overlook the harmony and symmetry of the cosmos. If I saw things in that way, would I lose the ability to stand in awe and humility of the world?

A. It may well be that from the perspective of physics and higher mathematics, the world we live is marvelous. I can see that side, as well. All I have to do is look up into the night sky and there is wonderment.

However, regardless of whether the universe is amazing, curious, strange or chaotic, the dilemma of your own life, your own universe demands a human perspective. You are a sentient being with a mind and body. If you look as carefully at this body and mind as you have at the universe you will see irony, see the bewildering, and see the bizarre nature of our predicament. You may then wish, like me, to solve the puzzle. There is where the Path the Buddha pointed to comes in.

Q. When I meditate on a mantra, a ringing sound comes into the mind which often overrides the mantra and pushes it into the background. What is this ringing sound I hear? Is it normal?

A. It is quite normal to hear that sound. That sound is there continuously but we rarely turn our attention towards it. When we do, it amplifies from a faint hum to a roaring sound. Some meditators believe that ringing sound is existential resonance. I believe it is the residue of the energy that arose out of the

"Big Bang". Astrophysicists now believe that there is lingering radiation from the Big Bang which can be identified and measured. They talk in terms of light and radioactivity. I believe it is the same energy recognized as the relentless sound in our minds. When we subdue the noise and the mind becomes tranquil, the usual mind stuff and mind static goes out of the picture. Then, we can hear that sound.

Q. **I have a problem with sleepiness. Right from the first times I meditated, in just a few minutes I would slump down and fall asleep while sitting. I have never been able to cure the problem.**

A. I recommend that you walk back and forth quickly for at least 10 minutes as a warm up before every sitting session. After walking quickly, walk naturally for another 5 minutes or so. Don't think that this is wasting meditation time. The walking should also be done with mindfulness. I don't think you will be able to walk and sleep at the same. At least, I can't.

After this "warm-up", come to the sitting posture. You will find that your sitting will have some vitality. When the drowsiness begins to overtake you, repeat the walking remedy. It will take a while before you can sit for 20-30 minutes without nodding off. But this is the way to challenge and overcome the obstacle of drowsiness.

Right now, the problem of sleepiness has established itself. So, when you go to sit you don't have any confidence you can overcome this heavy energy. And so the situation continues deepening. Follow these instructions and soon you will be sitting with a bright mind.

Q. **Is it true that we have soul mates and what is the best way to find them?**

A. It is true. Probably there are many around. But I wouldn't be in too big a hurry to meet one. The popular view is that a soul mate is someone so special, so magical that meeting this person would immediately transform our lives. Life would be like living on a fluffy white cloud, having a birthday everyday, and subsisting on nothing but ice cream and pizza. It would be heaven-realm time. Every moment filled with sensual happiness and unremitting bliss.

We Buddhists are much more sober concerning re-uniting with old lovers. We see it as the next episode in a saga. There is work yet to be done. We unite with our soul mates in order to join forces, to collaborate in order to develop the attributes needed to see things clearly to fully mature as a human being. This process is difficult. It's not about ice cream and pizza at all. It is a much more intense and daunting relationship than we could expect from an ordinary relationship. It would likely involve illness, trust issues, confrontations with deeply ingrained fears, etc. These relationships are fertile soil to propel us through many demanding lifetimes in just one.

Q. **My wife and I constantly fight with each other about just about everything. Our marriage is a deeply committed one and our disagreements and arguments are not fought with malice. So, the option of divorce isn't in the cards. This situation just seems to be karma that entwines us. What can be done about this?**

A.   You're right that it is karma. The problem would dissolve immediately if you had the generosity to capitulate to your wife's points. Or, the other way round. Generosity is the primary virtue that produces peace. All your relationship needs is for one of you to let go. What does it matter who is right? Is "right" empirical? Think hard about this.

Q.   **Even though my husband and I work hard to give our kids a comfortable life and the opportunity to study to whatever level they wish, they walk around looking miserable and forlorn. We can sympathize that the world of our kids looks far gloomier than when we were young. Still, they have to accept things as they are and make the best of their lives. We just don't know what to do to help them through the "teenage funk". This is not just a problem for my family but for most of the families in our suburb. Some kids in my son's high school have committed suicide. Some, like my daughter, just spend a lot of time in their rooms watching TV and playing games. I encouraged them to do a meditation course and a yoga course for young adults, but they are not receptive. Do you have any suggestions?**

A.   The attitudes you are talking about come about when people think too much only about themselves. The constant proliferation on "me", "me", "me" and "my happiness", "my happiness", "my happiness" anchors the mind in an untenable situation. People caught in this totally self-centered mind environment worry about themselves all the time. Even small problems get blown up into an impossible predicament. From their desperation, even suicide becomes a viable option.

For the sake of their sanity, they need to go out and help other people. They need to take themselves out of their self-centered world and volunteer to serve others. Every community has groups of kind-hearted people offering their time and energy to worthy causes. If you can guide them in that direction their whole demeanor would quickly change. They help others. In helping others they help themselves. Everybody wins.

Q.   **As part of an international sales team I fly around a lot. Too much. When I was younger, I could cope with the jet lag, and general malaise one gets from flying long distances. Still, I need the job. I really need to improve my physical stamina and psychological state if I am to keep up with the younger guys on the team. I have tried herbal jet lag remedies, sleeping pills, eating on-board and not eating on board. It all comes down to the same lethargic feeling that lingers for days.**

A.   Some years ago, at the request of several air hostesses, I wrote a little book with tips on how to deal with the long-haul lifestyle. Apart from suggesting they take a de-tox kit with them wherever they go, I didn't write too much about medicines, food, entertainment, or caffeine. One's intuition will guide us to act intelligently.

What I did advocate is that they pack a sleeping mat, blanket, fresh cotton clothing, and a meditation cushion along with them on every trip. When they arrive at their hotel they should bathe, change into comfortable lightweight clothing, take their meditation cushion into one corner of the room, light a small candle (so as not set off the fire detector) and sit quietly for 20-30 minutes. Hotel rooms accumulate weird energies from alcohol, snack foods, and love-less sex. The sitting brings an aura of protection to the lodger. After the sitting session, roll down the sleeping mat, roll up some clothes into a pillow, cover yourself with your own personal blanket and allow the body to rest naturally.

Those who followed these instructions told me they needed a lot less sleep, slept much better, and woke up refreshed and clear. Previously, some of them often had strange and unpleasant dreams. This isn't surprising considering how many people slept in that hotel bed. There was another section with instructions for sending loving-kindness to the whole team serving the aircraft and all the passengers as well. And another section providing basic yoga instructions.

You could do as they do and bring your own sleeping mat, mini-pillow, and meditation cushion. I guarantee you that just this will effectively solve your problem.

Interestingly, I began thinking about this several years ago when an air hostess visited and told me about having nightmares after a strange night in a 5-star hotel. After a difficult long haul flight, she just put her things in the closet, pulled the blankets down and plopped into a heavy, disturbed sleep full of bizarre dreams. Seven o'clock the next morning there was a knock at her door. When she opened it she met the hotel manager, several security people and 3 or 4 policemen. It seems that the previous occupant disappeared and they wanted to check the room for clues. When they looked under the bed they found him dead.

Q. **For many years now I have been in and out of relationships. That's not because I don't want to be in a long-term meaningful relationship.**

A. You may be trying to put the cart before the horse. If you have yet to have a meaningful relationship with yourself, that is, with Truth, you are not going to have a meaningful relationship with anyone else. To have a meaningful relationship with yourself means to know why you are born, what your duties are, what karma is and what it means in your life, and what needs to be cultivated within us in order to come to the end of confusion and dissatisfaction.

If you haven't come to know these aspects, what can meaningfulness mean in relation to another?

Q. **Why do you wear that robe? If freedom is uppermost in your lifestyle, why don't you just wear nothing at all?**

A. These robes are simple garments. Easy to sew, easy to maintain, and they provide some protection from the sun, rain, insects, and cold. Personally, I would be at ease wearing nothing. However, many of you would feel uncomfortable with that dress code. So, the Buddha had us wear these robes for your sake.

Q. **So, if we all struggle for happiness, why do so few find it?**

A. The world and the Dharma run in opposite directions. Most people get it upside down. They believe happiness is in excitement and that happiness comes from accumulating things when in fact, the quiet mind is the doorway to Supreme Happiness. The Supreme Happiness I am talking about is the mind at Peace, the mind transformed through Dharma in the Heart. Most people become uneasy when the mind is quiet; they believe something is wrong. So they look for something to agitate it. They don't get it.

Q. **I find myself talking to myself about events that were never resolved in the past. Is that an indication that these events are trying to reconcile themselves?**

A. When you talk to yourself in this way, the speech function has gone off on automatic pilot. There is no awareness to guard or protect you. So, regardless of what you say out loud, there is the autopilot talking to a ghost. This is closer to a moment of insanity than intelligence working on your behalf. Things will work themselves best when the mind is abiding in silence. That is why we talk on and on about meditation.

Q. **I can see what needs to be done and I have faith in the Path you are pointing to but I have yet to do much in the way of real practice. I have plenty of suffering in my life. Should I go on a meditation retreat?**

A. Maybe. You won't lose anything by spending time in retreat. However, once you see the situation as it is and the way out, pursuing the way will occur naturally. Just as the self-survival mechanism keeps us alive, the sacred energy within you will direct you toward the end of suffering.

Q. **What is worse, hate or love?**

A. Interesting observation. As you already suspect, they are both dangerous conditions. The source of some hatred comes out of karma, some comes out of family and environmental situations… especially people we are in close proximity to. But the most negative emotions and malicious actions come out of love. Love would win the prize, for out of love comes jealousy, binding (opposing the desire to be free), hatred, revenge, etc. How many beings have been killed out of love for family, ethnicity, country, religion? How much destruction has occurred out of love for one's country? Your question is a very good one. It is something that everyone needs to understand through the eyes of Dhamma rather than the world. In seeing with clarity this thing we call "love", we come to realize the deceptive and confusing nature of "love" and the need for a spiritual anchor within ourselves.

Q. **Often after sitting and meditating for an hour, I feel depressed. On one hand, I would say the meditations are very calm, clear, well concentrated. But then, opening my eyes and moving along, I experience a strange sadness for which there is not any immediate cause. I am not sure if this is part of my purification process, or if possibly I am collecting negative energy from outside of me.**

A. It's exceptional that you take practice so seriously and have been observing what works for you and what doesn't. It is likely that the depression you experience after meditating is the sobering effect that comes from scrutinizing the mind. Normally, people relate to the world in a drunken modality, a kind of carbonated consciousness. A mentality that is searching and is primed for something to happen through the external sense receptors: romance, adventure, sport, etc. People who delight in the written word will feel glee when they come upon a turn of a phase that bumps up their state of mind. This illustrates how the mind, as a sense receptor, works in the same way. All of this, mind you, is the intention to get high. What you are experiencing through meditation is a reduction of that fuzziness as the mind drops down into its original serenity. This is what is known as "the original mind". The techniques you are employing will certainly bring you good results. However, I would recommend that before each sitting that you do some walking meditation for at least 10 minutes to bring energy into the body and mind.

Q. I would also appreciate a little confirmation concerning meditation techniques. I meditate for 40 minutes every morning. Usually I try to observe the incoming and outgoing breath at a point just below the nostrils. I conclude each meditation with sharing love and compassion with friends, family and all beings, sending out my calmness and joy mentally and through visualizing. Finally, along the lines that I have learned from Thich Naht Hahn, is to practice mindfulness throughout the day, cooking, walking, etc. Can you tell if I am on the right path? Am I missing any vital aspects of the practice? Is there any other technique that I should practice that will assist in my purification, clarity and development of my spiritual being?

A. Considering how many activities you have in your life and the amount of time you dedicate for meditation practice, I'd say you are doing fine. If you can add another session in the evening, that would help to clear out things that you may be holding onto or have not resolved through your interactions in the world. It would give you some more personal time. Also, you will find useful, the practice of trying to attend to minute details as you do your duties throughout the day.

Q. Last time I visited you I left with "Truth is how you feel" and that has stayed with me for over two years. I have since come across the statement that "intention is all that there is". I have some mixed experiences with this notion and its application.

A. Again, I will try and answer your question in non-technical terms. However, when we talk about the mind-ground, regardless of what terms we use, you must focus your attention to the best of your ability or the words will pass by like a freight train in the night. In the first place, obviously, the mind is always busy with the stuff of the mind -- thoughts, concepts, ideas, and all manner of proliferation. They are all there intact in their entirety right from the beginning. The stimulation which induces movement within the mind is happening on its own through the energy of the mind. Because of this activity and interaction, the mind invites the defilements (primarily anger, lust-greed, and ignorance) to associate with thought forms. This is the "given". Intention is an energy form that exists within the mind. If this were not so, where would it exist? When intention is activated it sucks up the mind stuff it craves thereby making that particular tack dominant. It has a bias. That bias is that which it has a propensity or predilection towards. And that depends on the character of the mind. A pure mind will produce intention. An impure mind will produce impure intention. The purity or impurity largely depends upon karma, "boon-bahp" (accumulated goodness and accumulated un-goodness). The intention has now generated something with dominating power we can call desire. From there this energy can motivate the body to act in a particular way. There is a mitigating force called mindfulness-awareness that can subdue this energy by overriding it. Mindfulness-awareness oversees the behavior of the mind including the desire-bound movement arising along with intention. This is our saving grace for without it, we would just be a slave of the reactions between mind stuff and intention. Once intention was set there would be no way to curb robotic behavior. Can we say that intention is everything? I don't think so, for there are all kinds of activated factors present along with intention. It is intention which selects, inclines and dominates. Action or inaction then follows, depending on the power and authority of mindfulness-awareness. So, in terms of dominant energies, intention is the top dog. However, we should understand the whole picture and the dynamics of mind.

Q.   **I don't want to sound impolite but I need to return home in a few hours so I have to leave now. I would like to be able to try what you have been talking about on the long haul flight back. I know nothing about meditation. I stumbled in here with my friend just because I needed to kill some time. However, after listening to this discussion I would like to know, briefly, how to refine the mind. What can I do on the way home to discover whether this meditation works or not?**

A.   I don't think you're impolite, just someone who doesn't give yourself much time to do anything other than follow the tour guides. O.K. To practice properly we must keep the 5 precepts, develop concentration and build up insight into "the-way-things-are". When you get on the plane, find your seat, and pin or tape a note "Do not disturb" on your shoulder. Close your eyes and come to a comfortable posture. Turn your complete attention toward and into your breath. That is your meditation object. That is where everything is to go. Do this until you need to use the toilet. In moving about, be aware of things as they are in the present reality. Then, come back to your seat and return to where you were. If you are diligent and keep your energy and concentration on the meditation object, something unexpected will happen. Perhaps you will find that the meditation object disappears into emptiness. You are to turn your complete attention to the emptiness. Let go of the idea of a self observing this phenomenon and just know without this "knowing" associating with anyone. Stay with this for as long as you are able to. When the energy here changes, turn your attention to trying to find yourself. Where are you? If there is really someone, a soul, an enduring entity, you should be able to see through the mind to that thing. If you have trouble sustaining this investigation, observe that everything changes and try and find two mind-moments that are identical. That will be a fascinating beginning for you. If this practice intrigues you, as it does me, you can continue on and I will offer you further advice as the occasion warrants.

Q. **Can you please offer me some knowledge on a recurrent thought that keeps telling me to look beyond my present state of being, not to the past or the future, but beyond my "state of being" - to see beyond this? I struggle with this concept and meditate on it but am not receiving any answers. Can you recommend how I can indeed seek this in myself? Thank you so very much.**

A. I have no idea what something beyond your "present state of being" could be about. Nevertheless, if there is such a dimension, it would have no bearing on our solving our human predicament. It is a trick being played by your defilements. Remember, the spiritual seeker is at war with the defilements. They are strong, clever, and will fight back down to the very last battle. Here is an example of an attempt to befuddle you. In Truth, you don't want to look beyond your present state of being. What else is real?

Even the defilements know that they can't delude you into believing you will find Truth in the past or future. So they invent something to baffle you and throw you into confusion. One thing that you can find good about this experience is that you are obviously on the right track or you wouldn't be encountering this kind of clever obstacle.

Q. **I have completed my Master's thesis and will graduate in a couple of weeks. Like everyone else in my world, I have been in schools for just about all of my life. And I seem to have gotten pitifully little for my time and effort. I really don't know anything about life outside of my greenhouse. My life is sheltered and protected. Still all kinds of painful, confusing and frustrating things happen to me and my friends. Obviously there is no way to be sheltered from hurt feelings, disappointment, a broken heart, idiotic behavior, uncontrollable reactions, etc. I think it's time now to learn about myself. I guess I have come to the point where I know something about the pattern of bumps and grinds in life. Would you recommend travel, reading books focusing on self-development, spirituality, philosophy, or what?**

A. First, I would like to praise you on recognizing your psychological and spiritual needs. Many people go from their university to a job, to family life, to senior citizenry in a kind of daze. You have taken keen interest in coming to understand more about your life. As I see it, it is everyone's duty to make sense out of the parade of events that rumble through our lives. Life is an unfolding Persian rug. We don't have a clue as to what is going to happen next. We can only accept our karma and prepare ourselves to meet the challenges. Religion is the tool which teaches us how to still the mind and contemplate the-way-things-are. It should challenge our assumptions, not reinforce them.

With inner reflection, the principles underlying our life become known. Principles such as the fact of change, the inevitability of pervasive unsatisfactoriness, the fact that whatever begins, ends, the fundamental (though overlooked) Truth of illness, old age, and death. So, how you come to realize Reality depends on your karmic predicament. You may have to travel around the world 20 times or simply visit a local hospital. You may need to read everything you can get your hands on in the personal development section of your university library or you might just enter into a star-crossed "love" relationship and, in 3 months, learn more about the-way-things-are than you would learn by reading every New Age book ever written. It all depends. Don't go crazy trying to make a decision concerning the direction of your life. Just maintain an uncompromising determination, do your duty, and the Teachings will come to you.

Q. **I met a woman in a bar some weeks ago who I like very much. Many of my friends have been warning me that relationships with bar girls are destined to be nothing but trouble. She is kind, trustworthy, and loves looking after me. I am thinking about asking her to marry me. Still, the advice from some good friends rings in my ear. I am talking about this to you because she is a good Buddhist. Almost every morning she offers food to the monks and on special days brings food to the temple. Apart from her occupation, everything about her is appealing.**

A. What she does and what she is can be two very different things. The ways you describe her along with your obvious attraction to her are positive signs. If you are asking for my advice, I would just suggest you cool down a bit and spend more time developing your friendship before rushing into a marriage. This is a matter of the Heart, you have to rely on your intuition. Lastly, from a

Buddhist perspective, I need to offer this for your reflection. The love you feel will certainly lead to suffering. Not because she has been working in a bar but because of love itself. Romantic love, inevitably, is the catalyst for suffering. Your friends are right, but for the wrong reason.

Q. **Just what is "Samadhti"? I have only practiced meditation with a book so I don't know if I have ever entered "Samadhti"?**

A. "Samadhti" occurs when the mind gathers into one point. It may establish itself weakly or strongly depending upon various factors. What is critical is that "sati (mindfulness-awareness)" is watching over the mind and there is neither wanting nor fear infecting the mind. The mind is at rest. You undoubtedly have entered this state; however you still distrust your capability and that factor has led to your confusion.

For your reflection, Samadhi is that which arises at the end of wanting. Vipassana, is that which arises at the end of attachment to thought.

Q. **What is the state of Enlightenment like?**

A. The notion of a personal self has been extricated, whereas ordinary people continually refer to the notion of who they think they are: there conditioning, experiences, culture, etc. all gather into this notion which is active in every relationship. Without the idea of a self there is simply a direct knowing of whatever impacts upon the senses. There is no fear, no wanting. There is freedom.

Q. **What part does astrology have in the Buddha's Teachings?**

A. Astrology is a technique for one's karmic inheritance. No doubt there is a certain variety of personality types. That could well have something to do with the stars. What I see is that these techniques are a kind of software which can freeze-frame the character, attitudes, inclinations, tendencies, etc. of a person thus providing a picture that can be studied apart from the distraction of so-call-real-life. And karma is the hardware. That is, karma is the inherent energies that need to be resolved and purified.

Q. **The other day I heard you advise one of your supporters to "just throw away your medicine". To me that sounds like a very rash and callous statement, considering how sick she is.**

A. It's because she is so sick and because I have a great amount of affection for her that I offered that advice. It is the nature of the body to heal itself. Medicine only interferes with the process and makes it more difficult. In order to give ourselves the best chance to heal, we need to meditate in order to strengthen the mind. A strengthened mind will invigorate the body. The body knows how to heal itself. It just needs the energy to do the job. You probably think this is a naive or simplistic approach to healing. You believe that when we are sick we need the right medicines to force the body to heal. With that approach the patient will only heal themselves in spite of the intervention of medicine. If you don't believe me, just ponder this---have you ever heard of a medicine that cured anything? Allow the body to heal naturally. Rest fully, sun bathe, moon bathe, take short walks, and fast. If a patient cannot fast completely, he/she should begin with only fruit juices for 2-3 months. After the cleansing phase, vegetables and solid healthy food can be eaten. I am only providing you with an overview. For more specifics and getting the timing right, a patient should be under the care of a natural healing professional.

Q.   **My experience is that chronic illness seems to linger on and on. Maybe we just tolerate it.**

A.   You're close to the truth. Many people come to cherish their illnesses because they have come to identify who they are through this prism.

Q.   **How can I cut down on the mistakes I make?**

A.   Why would you want to do that? You would miss out on all kinds of lessons. Mistake-making is the nature of life. We make mistakes from the beginning to the end. We learn from our mistakes. Without mistakes, without suffering and conflict, how would we learn? Actually, I recommend that my students not try to change anything. The energy for change is directed at reducing suffering. Don't reduce suffering…realize it.

Q.   **If that is true, what can we do to help someone suffering from illness?**

A.   The mind has power over the body, consciousness can heal. Not just the one we are using but others. The principle is that there is one mind and one body. In fact, there is a primary field encompassing all time and space. Our minds have the ability to immerse in this energy which is a pool of potentiality. In order to get there we need to jettison the notion of a self and the wanting and fear that's involved with that concept. Meditation, and its primary factor, attention, take us through the past and future and into the pool of presence. We arrive with an expanded awareness which we can point towards a "someone". The awareness that arrives here and dips into this energy of coherence turns up along with kindness and compassion. From this point, the energy we emanate is conducive to healing. We target the person who is out of harmony and diseased with the loving-healing energy from that source. And the healing works.

Q.   **I have been suffering from progressively worse arthritis for over 10 years. Sometimes the cramps cause so much pain that my eyes tear. Can meditation help with the pain?**

A.   Indeed. I will offer you one technique that you may scoff at, thinking it is just too simple to be effective. When the pain is developing, close your eyes and hold your breath for as long as you can. While you are holding your breath, turn your attention to the mind-ground of consciousness. Your mind will stop running around everywhere and the fear aspect will evaporate. Probably all sensation of pain will disappear immediately. What will be present is simply knows knowing. This simple technique is not only an effective way to pull the rug out from under pain but is also a Teaching in itself. You will see that when only- knowing is present, the personal notion you have of your body vanishes. With the lesson you learned from this experience you will have the energy to meditate in order to manifest this awareness-only state for hours at a time.

Q. **The different schools of Buddhism practice meditation in different ways. Are they equally effective in getting to Enlightenment?**

A. If they teach their disciples to live simply and morally, to establish concentration through the use of a meditation object, and to use the quiet mind to see the Nature of Reality (change, conflict, and no-self), they will be equally effective. That's the Path. Different schools enter it in distinctive ways.

Q. **What's the caveat? By that I mean what is the most imperative aspect in meditation?**

A. Keep the mind in the mind.

Q. **My daughter has been meditating for years. Today she managed to drag me here to meet you. I am surprised to find that I can understand what you are talking about and would like to learn how to meditate as well. Can you give me a brief synopsis of the procedure?**

A. I can provide you with a framework but it will only be words. The Buddha's Dhamma is something each of us needs to realize for themselves. You will have to move into it from a point of rational faith and find out for yourself what meditation is about. From the beginning understand that Buddhist meditation is about cultivating wisdom and compassion. That's all. It's not about anything particularly esoteric. In order to cultivate wisdom there must be a base for which wisdom can manifest itself. That base is a quiet mind. To quiet the mind we use a mantra or a point of reference. Everything that arises in consciousness we bring to that point of reference. When thoughts go into that point, or memories, or plans, etc. funnel into that point, they end there. This is bringing all the energies of the mind into one point. That is the end point of proliferation. Now we let go of the point of reference or mantra so that the mind can rest in its natural abiding. It is essential to quiet the mind in this way in order to develop wisdom. We say that mindfulness-awareness ("Sati") has subdued restless, vagrant proliferation. With the mind now gathered into itself, mindfulness-awareness attends to whatever arises in consciousness and sees that it is a changing condition, because it is changing there is discomfort, and that none of it belongs to anyone. Every mind-moment of this state of awareness increases the energy of the mind. In time, the invigorated wisdom that manifests recognizes what to keep, what to develop, what to reject and what to discard. The wisdom sees beyond the idea of an illusory self (a body and mind). It sees that there are just components in a state of flux and flow. At this stage the process develops deeper and deeper Realization of "the-way-things-are."

Q. **If I meditate in the morning, as you suggest, will my memory improve?**

A. Probably. Improvement in everything concerning the mind happens across the board. Your memory perks up, you make fewer mistakes, your appreciation of the situations you meet deepens, your physical health recovers, and your attitude towards work, your family and life improves. You will no longer take the natural suffering that comes from doing and confronting things as an insult. You won't hold on to things in the way you previously clung to unsatisfactory situations. If you do get angry at someone you will quickly see the transparent quality of opinions and grudges. You will quickly see that when things break or don't work properly that is what should be expected of the paraphernalia and machines we depend on. Overall, life is lighter and softer.

Q. **When someone has meditated as long and as hard as you have, what kind of transformation has happened to their mind?**

A. Their mind has dignity. The radiant power of the mind has relaxed into its own inherent strength. There is no wanting or fear. An elegant appreciation of life and its relationship to karma and Truth occurs.

Q. **What can I learn from meditation?**

A. If you practice properly you won't learn anything but you will unlearn a lot. The source of your problem in not being able to live in harmony with this world stems from what you have learned from others. Instead of following your intuition you have learned to be led and bound by the rules given by others and by your habits, habits which are mainly dominated by self-interest and social conventions. After you have flushed out these ideas your mind will return to its original purity. Actually, the mind is always pure; it's the ideas and notions that you have been trained to cherish that are in conflict with "the-way-things-are".

Q.   I heard you tell someone that he didn't need periodic retreats. Don't you think retreats are beneficial? I always feel invigorated after a retreat.

A.   I think I remember the context of that conversation. I suggested he back off from his addiction to meditation retreats. Some people who live for the times they are on retreat miss out on the long periods in between. They don't recognize that the possibility to develop is with them in every single present moment, and that practice should develop in every place, at all times until retreat time and ordinary everyday life time are seen as essentially the same thing.

Q   What's the point of meditation?

A.   It's the same point as all of our other activities---striving for Happiness. Happiness in the mind is much superior to happiness of the body. And the highest happiness in the mind is the Happiness of a peaceful mind.

Q.   Ajahn, I believe my wishes are similar to the desires of all the other people I know. I want a good job, a good wife, good family, good kids, good house and the like. Does this wanting trigger the suffering that won't go too far away? Is everyone going for the wrong thing? And if so, how can anyone live without these desires?

A. The menu of things you want will certainly generate suffering in your life. The suffering is in direct to relationship to the degree of intense greed and ignorance. This factor, coupled with your attachments, determines the magnitude of your suffering. For instance, loving somebody will cause a great deal of suffering. This is because love is an intense emotion which galvanizes all kinds of wanting.

Examine the issue for yourself and you will see that since you hold on to your catalog of desires, you will certainly experience disappointments, you will experience frustration at the slow pace of advancement toward getting what you what (we have to endure the "getting what we don't want" first), along with a churning array of doubts all triggered because of your clinging to wanting.

Q. **So the problem is the attachment to my desires?**

A. Actually, at the deepest level the problem is that you believe you are who you think you are. Whenever there is a person acting in this fashion your space-time relationship to the world is always going to be future oriented. You are not present, so you are vulnerable. If you were to let go of being someone, you would be ever-present. In the present, there is no suffering. In the present, there is no person. What is it that can stick to no one?

The gist of your questions involve wondering if it is possible that everyone is off course, with what I said in mind, what do you think?

Q. **My good friend's wife has been diagnosed with cancer. He is reeling. Is there anything I can do for him?**

A. I have seen time and time again people living their life, enjoying concerts, sports, events, trips to the parks and beaches until one day someone close to them gets very ill or they themselves end up in an emergency room or ICU.

Like most people, even the friends and supporters of this Buddhist Way Place pretty much carry on with their lives with little concern for the inevitable reality of illness, old age and death. Some buy life insurance, but that's the extent of their preparation for the unavoidable.

So, when something overwhelms their emotions or threatens the images of the future, they come apart; reeling and trembling with no refuge to provide comfort.

Is there something you can do to diminish the fear, the desperation, and the sense of unfairness your friend is feeling? Probably not. If he had been practicing meditation he would have developed an understanding of the fragility and vulnerability of our lives. And the inevitability of separation from loved ones. Any meditator will come to understand very early in his/her practice that illness, aging, and death inevitably follow birthing. Once born, the rest of the cycle must follow. So when these things happen there is no shock. Our spiritual insight has prepared us to accept the predestined.

It's certainly not too late for your friend and his partner to begin to understand the nature of life. Everyone must do the work themselves. No one can do it for another. This fruit of meditation practice, unlike other things, does not deteriorate and is not limited to just this lifetime.

Q. **You continually talk about Wisdom and the functioning of Wisdom. It all sounds too abstract. Can you give me a concrete example?**

A. O.K. here is an example. Last week someone entered my hut and stole some batteries, a flashlight, an mp3 player, pens, tools, candles, etc. The need to make some kind of decision arose right then and there. How, or better, from where do we make our decisions? I could clean up the mess and forget about the incident or I could try and find out who did it and try and recover the things that were lost. I could live without the stolen stuff. I could live without almost anything. I decided that since the things stolen were gifts from supporters I had a duty to try and recover them. I tracked down the kid who stole these things. Actually when I found his house I couldn't find him but his relatives next door went into his room and returned some of the things they found under his mattress. I could have left it at that. There was another factor involved: this boy had stolen similar items 2 years earlier. Back then, I tracked him down, brought him to his school and I, the school principal, and the village headman gave him a talk on the evils of stealing. He listened to us in a disinterested fashion and then asked for forgiveness (a practice customarily used in Buddhist cultures). The boy was 11 years old. Even if I wanted to have the police deal with him he was 6 years under-age and could not be sent to a juvenile detention center or even detained in the local lock-up. This kid was quite savvy and knew that he was, in a way, beyond the law. Two or three days later a group of motorcycle guys on a Sunday Rally took a breather at this Wat to cool down their bikes and to ask questions concerning Buddha-Dhamma. I decided that these guys riding choppers and wearing outer space type helmets could frighten this kid more than the police, me, or the school principle. I asked them to take a ride over to his house and tell him that if he steals again, they would be back to drag him around and around the village until their rope burned out. That should have been the end of it, no? I'm illuminating this story for you to see that decisions were required all along and these decisions come out of the natural wisdom *beyond our minds*, to whatever extent we have any.

Fast forward to last week. Another theft with the same modus operandi. This time I ask the police to investigate the situation. This required another decision and like the earlier ones came out of an assessment based on wisdom. The police had no problem finding the thief using the police strategy of rounding up the "usual suspects". The culprit is still underage so the police bring him to me. What to do? The kid knows of his immunity, the police know of his immunity and so do I. He tells us that he sold the batteries, the flashlights, the tools to buy liquor and cigarettes. The police have gotten his confession concerning 8 other thefts in Wats adjacent to the village. He also smugly confesses that he stole metal from an electronics factory near by. He quit school last year and has not looked for any honest work. This boy is more professional than a seasoned thug and has long exploited his pre-adolescence.

Now he is sitting in front of me, the two policemen behind him and my attendant next to him. What to do? If I think about it adding in all the factors I would certainly end up mired in doubt and uncertainty. This boy's actions are those of a demon from hell. Stealing from the Buddha in order to buy whiskey is simply not human behavior. Still, he is a victim of his karmic condition. Most of his actions are pre-destined. His father died and his mother ran off leaving no forwarding address. His uncle acts as a guardian and he is drunk 24/7. There is no way to digest all the factors and arrive at a perceptive answer. My duty is to act judiciously, depending upon the storehouse of Wisdom that has arisen from my practice in order to do that which is appropriate to the situation. If I *let go* of my own ideas, my own experience, my emotions, in order to allow whatever wisdom I have built up the situation will be met intelligently. I am absolutely confident only wisdom can guide us to initiate the right action. What would you do? In a month, I may tell you what my accumulated wisdom prompted me to do.

Q. When I was younger I could run around and do just about anything. I hardly ever drank, never smoked, and rarely used recreational drugs. These days I am in middle age with a bit of a beer belly. I still run the same course but the amount of pleasure I get from it all is significantly less than it used to be, even with Viagra and wine. Is this because my senses have deteriorated?

A. Obviously, you still think pleasure is a function of the body. Actually, the pleasure anyone can get from their body is minimal. The pleasure you used to get and the pleasure you crave must involve an attitude of the mind.

As for the disappointment you are speaking about, the experience has changed due to the "diminishing returns" factor built into every pleasurable activity. The more you do the same or similar activity, the less pleasure you can get from it. In fact, if you were to do the thing you like to do the most continuously, it wouldn't be long before you would hate doing it! You may discover the bad news I was once shocked to discover and that is that everything that is, is prone to boredom.

Q. **My life situation is only confusion and chaos.**

A. There is no problem with the circumstances of your life. The problem is with the lack of awareness dampening down your Light. You are looking at the outer covering, the stuff that sustains the wheel of becoming. The circumstances of your life are not the same thing. What is going on in the body and mind is only the business of the body and mind. The body is not you.

Q. **I have read your books and translations which I find very useful. I, too, am a writer. I would like to know something about your writing process. Do you get up in the morning and get right on with last nights work?**

A. Not at all. I am a meditator first, a writer third. My writing is empowered by my meditation. If I just sat in front of a computer, followed my thinking and continuously hit keys, I know that I wouldn't be able to communicate anything of significance. Thought can never lead to Truth. There would just be cold-blooded symbols on a white page. Actually, I begin my morning by sitting and walking while simply observing my mind and body. My emphasis is focusing on my feelings. Not trying to change anything, and without any desire to try and get anything. I keep letting go of everything while I observe whatever is happening with absolute honesty. In this way, what I write is not an exercise in creativity, and not an event which reinforces ego. By the way, what am I secondly? Just a human being watching the sun cross the sky, the moon slip over the horizon, and the seasons change.

Q.   **I can see my thoughts but don't really see what is the value of seeing my thoughts.**

A.   The profound value of observing your thoughts is that you recognize that you are not your thoughts. If you can watch thoughts, how can you be thought? You pull yourself out of the world of thought and the slavery of following thoughts. If you are able to differentiate between being lost in thought and observing thought, you have clearly stepped on the Path to your freedom.

Q.   **You teach that practicing is not hard. I see it as demanding the strength of a superman. Who in this world can set up the kind of discipline that checks the mind and feels what is happening in the body? We are all habitually drunk on going along and acting on our thoughts.**

A.   It may seem like the advice that I am talking about is demanding too much. Sure, developing a discipline in our life requires effort and confidence. Sure, every spiritual Path requires a binding commitment to morality. Sure, we need to reign in the thought process through Samadhi. This is the way it is. There is only one way out of this, so everyone of us has to go against the grain and bring to an end the slavery of being fooled by machinery unrelated to who we really are. The thoughts in the mind are not us. When you finally get this you certainly will not want to be pulled by the nose into states of mind such as regret, jealousy, vengeance, lust, greed and utterly ridiculous beliefs. My motivation for talking about these things is to provide you with the very best opportunity to take yourself from a world of temporary, foolish happiness to a world of genuine bona fide Happiness. To help remove you from the burdens of being a person, of worrying about the future, of regretting the past, of hopes, of the search for more experience and more study (because you're good enough) and even the dream of becoming Enlightened. No one can release you from your heavy burden. No one can give you that freedom; you have to discover things-as-they-are for yourself.

Q. **What is the difference between other religions and Buddhism? I know only that Buddhism doesn't believe in a God?**

A. There are factors that are identical in Buddhism and theistic religions. You probably recognize that all religions revere morality and ethics. That's basic for the formation of a spiritual mind. And, actually, we could eliminate differentiation on the basis of whether Buddhism recognizes the existence of a God by saying that the God of Buddhism is Nature. But that is not an important factor. When we gather together the facets of all the various religions we notice that they are all saying pretty much the same thing using different words. However, the significant aspect of the Buddha's Teachings and the teachings of other teachers is that the Buddha's genius was able to see that the mind doesn't belong to us.

Q. I find that it's impossible for me to be mindful all the time. In fact, after all these years, I only have sporadic moments of mindfulness. What can I do?

A. You can't do anything about it! There is nothing for you to do. What you are experiencing is reality. The mind is like that. It is a changing thing and operates under the power and authority of change. It is not ours, not personal. It is under the power of non-self. Come to recognize when you are not aware, when you are asleep. That, too, is awareness. Be aware of your judgment, your thinking that you should be able to do something that no one can do. That is a fatal obstacle.

Q. So what does Nibbana feel like? I think it must be when the Heart is completely non-violent. And there is only emptiness.

A. Find out for yourself. It's something you can aspire to and accomplish. About all I can tell you are what factors are present in the Enlightened state and what factors are absent. Then, you use the time-tested tactics to put it all together. What disappears is wanting, mental proliferation, conflict and suffering, hesitation and doubt, as well as the notion that you are who-you-think-you-are; i.e. the body and the mind. What evolves is the absence of the idea that one is a body and mind. When the self mirage disappears, there is nothing for conflict, suffering, or unsatisfactoriness to stick into. Therefore, that accomplishment eliminates all suffering. As there is only true knowing, mental and physical phenomenon is merely observed. The whole process stops at knowing. There are no building things out of memory, out of desire, out of fear, out of hope, or comprises leading to a taste of pleasure. Both happiness and unhappiness are equal.

Non-violence is the way to Nibbana. Wisdom is the objective. The end of spinning on the wheel of never-ending re-birth is right at Wisdom. When the mind wants nothing, it automatically enters into the Heart. When wanting comes to the end point, freedom arises. There cannot be nothingness. The mind is never empty. Activity is the inherent nature of the mind.

Q. **At what point can I cut out all the compulsive and stupid thinking I can see afflicting me?**

A. It's not a point, so much as it's an attitude and a perspective. Practice to know what it's like to know things through feeling (not thought). Then stop at knowing. That will shut down the opportunity for mental proliferation to take you into suffering, into conflict. It can all end at awareness.

Q. **I must confess that I have not been interested in spirituality for very long. I have only restarted doing yoga and meditation for the past 5-6 months. Still, I am very keen on developing my awareness of what you call "knowing-the-way-things-are". Right now everything going through my mind appears murky, and obscure. I just can't get my mind around important spiritual concepts and can't quite connect the dots concerning various psychological relationships. What can I do to grasp spiritual knowledge faster?**

A. It feels like you are beginning to do the right things. At the root of your development you need to maintain ethical purity. That means that you should maintain the five precepts impeccably.

Endeavor to maintain a lifestyle incorporating non-violence as the nucleus of your life.

As I have often instructed, continue to observe the body and mind in the present moment. Whatever arises is what there is. Don't try to change anything. Just know things as they are.

You can't make the mind develop faster than its spiritual capability. Karmic energies, which you are helpless to change, play an important role. You can only do what needs to be done in the present and nurture your mindfulness. Whatever plane the mind has been brought to, that is the maximum stage of your development right now. That is where you are…it marks the frontier as to what you are entitled to discern. Increase the purity and energy of your mind, and your capability increases proportionally.

Closing moments

After 20 years here in this cave I have come to see most of the problems that plague people. First, I had to see them clearly in myself so right now they jump out when I first meet others. Essentially, the big issues hounding human beings are the search for Happiness (fused with meaning) and the depression that comes from a life devoid of meaning. Then, there is the ubiquitous confusion and frustration in people's minds as to what to do, how to do it and where to do it. Difficulties arise from lack of confidence, lack of guidance and a glut of doubt. Also, there is the matter of not recognizing and meeting the responsibilities we have in this life. When we don't honor these responsibilities properly, life becomes more and more difficult, less and less happy. We betray the opportunities we have been given with this human birth. When we observe carefully, we all can see that this is a realm where some happiness is possible and a variety of relentless suffering is guaranteed. The questions you encountered throughout this book exhibit this fact. They are human concerns, human modes of suffering we are all familiar with. If you haven't figured it out yet, I hope this final bit will help you to recognize that this world is precisely the best kind of environment for spiritual development. People think that suffering is evil so they try and run away from it. Actually, ironically, without suffering there would be no growth. The questions posed are the perfect medium for deepening and expanding awareness. A significant quantity of suffering ignites spiritual inquiry. Too much suffering, however, is crushing.

Many of us are in a position to get a great deal out of this incarnation. We just mistake (mis-take) our situation and maintain a constant state of distraction until it's time to die. We overlook the fact that the Happiness we crave can be attained through utilizing our life energy in the service of awakening. When the energy becomes sufficiently refined the obstacles are cleared away, the big prize, the encompassing Happiness that comes from a Peaceful mind arises naturally and automatically. Putting it all into words is rather easy. What is demanded, however, is not beyond our ability.

Embedded in the Thai culture we have a very elegant relationship which exists between Bhikkhus and lay people. The lay people support the practice of the monks as well as the fruits that arise out of their dedicated effort, determination, and sacrifice. After decades of meditation practice some monks will provide opportunities for meditation retreats under their personal guidance. Some will accept invitations to give Teaching by way of formal talks or casual conversations. Some will stay in a secluded environment and simply watch the grass grow and the seasons change. Some, like me, will write books. It depends upon one's karma. Here I would like to specifically acknowledge the foundation supporters whose offerings made this book possible. May the goodness of their generosity lead them to Peace, the Ultimate Happiness.

Khunying Somjit Insee

M.R. Chumjit Watanakhom

Pipath & M.R. Chorjit Bunnag

Voramon Bunnag

Narim Bunnag

Rueshanit Bunnag

Kasipol Ratanapassa

Luenyot Leelachart

Anongnard Leelachart

Prapas Kianpotiramard

Seefa Kianpotiramard

Surin Kittitornkun

Kanit Kittitornkun

Kosol, Ngahmpis and Krippong Wongsurawat

Dr. Ratanakuma